JESUS,
THE TREASURE
OF HEAVEN

Jesus,
The Treasure
of Heaven

A Devotional
for Any Season

Written by Susan-Louise Henning

LUMINARE PRESS

WWW.LUMINAREPRESS.COM

Jesus, The Treasure of Heaven: A Devotional for Any Season, 15 Weeks of Morning and Evening, 210 People, Places, and Things in the Bible That All Link to Jesus

Scripture from this publication is quoted from the Holy Bible, King James Version (KJV) and most of it is copied directly from: https://www.holybooks.com/wp-content/uploads/2010/05/The-Holy-Bible-King-James-Version.pdf

The preaching and teaching ministries of my local church were very helpful to me while writing this devotional. The ESV Study Bible and gotquestions.org were my study sources for content and context.

Got Questions Ministries, articles accessed between July 2019 and September 2021. [https://www.gotquestions.org]

Printed in the United States of America

Luminare Press
442 Charnelton St.
Eugene, OR 97401
www.luminarepress.com

LCCN: 2022912427
ISBN: 978-1-64388-816-3

For my daughter,
Holly

Contents

Why Is Jesus the Treasure of Heaven?

Jesus knows our sinful rebellion and loves us, so he invites us to repent of our sin and be reconciled to God by faith in his name because our sin leads to eternal death. Faith is a gift from God for all who diligently seek and embrace his only Son, the Lord and Savior, Jesus Christ.

Repentant people desire to turn from sin, toward Jesus. Jesus freely replaces our personal sin with his righteousness. The Father sent the Son to live and die without sin, so that the Holy Spirit may replace our sinful, temporary body with a righteous, spiritual body empowered to be rescued from death. Rebellious, repentant sinners are reconciled to God by faith in Jesus's name.

Jesus fulfilled a promise made to a tiny family that grew into a great nation, a promise first made in the garden of Eden. Jesus is the promised Messiah whose eternal kingdom consists of new heavens and a new earth in which righteousness dwells. God's kingdom is coming because King Jesus was crucified, rose victoriously from the grave, and reigns as Lord of heaven and earth.

Jesus offers hope for us to receive a resurrected, spiritual body just like he has; righteous, glorious, indestructible, imperishable, and suitable for eternal habitation with holy God. The Bible is God's love story, declaring Jesus from cover to cover. Jesus is our prophet, our priest, our king, our husband, our brother, our friend, our judge, our justifier, our rock, and more.

Therefore, Jesus is the treasure of heaven.

About the Author—
a Brief Testimony

When I was nineteen years old, God used a funeral, a television miniseries, and a horror movie to get me thinking about the Bible. My grandmother Louise Campanella said that the Bible is God's Word. Grandma was a credible source and she made me memorize Genesis 1:1 as a child.

At age nineteen, I started reading in Revelation and became confused. I turned to Genesis and read up to chapter twenty-two where God told Abraham to sacrifice his beloved son, Isaac. I shut the Bible and said, "NO!"

Thankfully, God used my Aunt Sarah Campanella-Griffin to encourage me to keep reading. God spared Abraham's son and provided a substitution for the sacrifice, so that Isaac would live. Aunt Sarah explained that God sent Jesus to the cross as the substitute to die in my place.

I asked God to forgive my sin and give me saving faith, so I may live eternally in Jesus's name. Each day I marvel that I am an undeserving sinner, saved by grace, working out my own salvation with fear and trembling. Now the Holy Spirit lives in my heart, God's security, until Jesus returns, or I go to heaven.

A month after I came to faith, I married Glen Henning. Then we welcomed our only child, Holly. Over thirty years have passed, and our daughter is married and raising her own family. The best legacy that I can leave to my beautiful daughter is this published testimony of my love for Jesus.

Chapter 1

Genesis
{1:1} In the beginning
God created the
heaven and the earth.

Adam

1 Corinthians {15:22} For as in Adam all die,
even so in Christ shall all be made alive.

THE BOOK OF GENESIS DESCRIBES GOD'S LOVING INTENtion for the creation of humanity. Adam was the first living soul created in God's image, the man who would influence humanity. God provided every good thing for Adam. In the garden of Eden, everything was good, there was no sin, no death, no shame. Best of all, there was free fellowship with loving God.

God gave Adam and Eve free will to trust and obey; both were free to disobey. God placed a tree in the garden, called the "tree of the knowledge of good and evil." God commanded Adam not to eat from this tree, because if he did, he would die.

God's enemy, the serpent, styled the fruit from the tree as an offer to advance humanity to be wise like God. He twisted God's words and challenged God's goodness for withholding such a beneficial fruit. Eve was tricked. Adam willfully ate in rebellion, bringing the curse of the law, which is sin and death.

Adam and Eve were exiled from the garden; however, their loving God clothed them with animal skins, the first sign of the shedding of blood for the forgiveness of sins.

Jesus planned from eternity to fix Adam's fallen fellowship due to the sin problem by perfectly keeping every law, so to exchange sinful flesh for a righteous life worthy to be reconciled to holy God. The second Adam, the sinless Son, became sin, tasted death, was vindicated by God, declared holy, raised from the dead, and given the name above all names, Jesus. One day, every knee will bow, and every tongue confess that Jesus is Lord.

John the Baptist

*Matthew {11:2} Now when John had heard in the
prison the works of Christ, he sent two of his disciples,
{11:3} And said unto him, Art thou he that should come,
or do we look for another? {11:4} Jesus answered and
said unto them, Go and shew John again those things
which ye do hear and see: {11:5} The blind receive their
sight, and the lame walk, the lepers are cleansed, and
the deaf hear, the dead are raised up, and the poor have
the gospel preached to them. {11:6} And blessed is [he,]
whosoever shall not be offended in me.*

IN ISAIAH 40:3-5, JOHN THE BAPTIST'S LIFE WAS FORETOLD;
this was about seven hundred years prior to his birth. John
put God first, told others about the Messiah, and sought Jesus
when in doubt.

Baptism is symbolic of washing away sin under water and
rising to a new life of repentance. Many Jews were baptized
because they knew that John was a great prophet. Prophets
delivered God's Word to the people. John baptized Jesus to
identify Jesus with sinful flesh. John's role was to exalt Jesus
and abate himself; however, even the best Christ exalters can
doubt during distress.

The offense of prison created doubt regarding Jesus's credibility. John needed to know of Jesus's works, and that heaven
is a spiritual kingdom. Jesus testified that John was the greatest prophet, the last one to look for the Messiah.

May this be a lesson to believers seeking Jesus when in doubt.
Exalt Jesus in all things, so bouts with doubt may be brief.

The Curse

Romans {8:2} For the law of the Spirit of life in Christ Jesus hath made me free from the law of sin and death.

IMAGINE WHAT LIFE WOULD BE LIKE WITHOUT THE CURSE. There would be no death, no pain, no worries. Life without the curse was the best thing about the garden of Eden because there was free fellowship with holy God for humanity. Matthew 29:46 assures that humanity is guilty of sin, and unrepentant sin leads to God's judgment of eternal death.

The book of Genesis reveals how Eve lingered by the only forbidden tree in the garden. The enemy tempted Eve by questioning God's trustworthiness. When Adam willfully ate from the forbidden tree he sinned, and a curse entered our world. The curse is the law of sin and death for humanity and the world. God desires reconciliation and restoration because of his great love; however, his righteous requirement binds humanity to obey every holy law—an impossible demand apart from Jesus's finished work at the cross.

Part of sharing the gospel is explaining the curse. God must punish rebellion because he is holy. The gospel of redemption begins with mankind's rebellion that caused the fall from holiness and eternal life. The curse leads to eternal death; however, faith in Jesus leads to eternal life.

When people understand the curse the gospel promise becomes clear. God does not want sinful humanity to inherit eternal death. God the Father freely and graciously gives repentant sinners faith in the Son for eternal life. Jesus cured the curse at the cross because the demand for human righteousness, by obedience to the perfect law, is satisfied in him.

David

*Ezekiel {11:19} And I will give them one heart, and
I will put a new spirit within you; and I will take
the stony heart out of their flesh, and will give them
an heart of flesh.*

BEING GRATEFUL TO GOD, HAVING GENUINE SORROW OVER personal sin, possessing confidence in the Holy Spirit, and desiring to be loyal to Jesus are all characteristics of a person with genuine faith in the God of the Bible. John 6:44 confirms that apart from the effective grace of God, no one has the desire, drive, or determination to acquire a heart that seeks after God the Father in heaven.

David was known to be the man after God's own heart. Although David was a sinful man and made regretful decisions throughout his life, he was truly repentant when he sinned against God. David served God as a shepherd, a warrior, was king of Israel, and was highly favored by the Lord. God promised to establish David's throne and give it to the Messiah forever. As a king, David was blessed with great political power; however, he understood that the promised Messiah would not just be considered a royal descendant, but the Messiah would be David's Lord.

Psalm {110:1} The LORD said unto my Lord, Sit thou at my right hand, until I make thine enemies thy footstool.

Through the receiving of the Holy Spirit, by faith in Jesus, believers are given a new heart, a heart like David had for God. Believers acquire a heart like David only by faith in Jesus.

Noah

John {10:1} Verily, verily, I say unto you, He that entereth not by the door into the sheepfold, but climbeth up some other way, the same is a thief and a robber.

BETWEEN THE TIME THAT GOD REMOVED ADAM AND EVE from the garden of Eden and the account of the great flood, the immoral behavior of the people on earth became grievous to God. God's plan was to judge and purge the world with a great flood.

Genesis chapter 6 says that only Noah found favor with God, because he was blameless in his generation. Noah was the first person in the Bible called righteous by God because he walked with God. Noah, through his faith and obedience to God, built the ark. Noah's act of faith and obedience in building the ark and saving the lives that God brought to him was a direct foreshadow of the Lord Jesus.

Everything that did not enter by way of the door God provided in the ark perished from the face of the earth, this was God's sovereign will. God showed believers through the record of Noah that without God humankind will do nothing but bad all the time and God will judge them.

The rainbow of promise, found in Genesis 9:8-16, reminds that human rebellion will never again be punished in the flood of death by water. The Son of promise, sent by the Father, reminds that human rebellion is punished by the flood of precious blood at the cross. Like Noah's door was the only way to preserve life, Jesus's door is the only way to eternal life. Have you entered in?

The Blood

*Matthew {26:27} And he took the cup, and gave
thanks, and gave [it] to them, saying, Drink ye all of
it; {26:28} For this is my blood of the new testament,
which is shed for many for the remission of sins.*

SIN IS EXPENSIVE TO FORGIVE BECAUSE OF THE HOLINESS
of God. God refuses sin, punishes sin, and condemns sinners to eternal death. Only Jesus has a righteous standing
before God.

There is no hope for the sinner to stand before God without faith in our Lord and Savior, Jesus Christ. The reason for
our hope of righteousness has to do with Jesus's blood. Under
the Mosaic law, priests would quickly sacrifice the unblemished animal to obtain the lifeblood.

The priests used the blood for the purification of themselves and God's people. God lovingly ordained this exchange
to allow an innocent life to atone for the guilty life, so that
guilty sinners could temporarily come before holy God with
a righteous standing and a pure heart.

The lifeblood from the animals could only make a temporary atonement for sin. Jesus's plan involved a permanent
solution to the problem of sin. Jesus's shed blood at the cross
permanently made atonement for the sins of all who believe.

Unlike the direction to the priest to mercifully empty the
lifeblood of the animal to secure God's atonement, the plan
for God's Son was to be less merciful. When the time came for
the Son of God to be lifted on the altar of the cross, to shed
his lifeblood as a ransom, Jesus was fully wounded.

Gomer

Isaiah {53:6} All we like sheep have gone astray; we have turned every one to his own way; and the LORD hath laid on him the iniquity of us all.

TRUE LOVE AND MARRIAGE ARE THE VERY PICTURE OF THE relationship between the Lord Jesus Christ and the church. The faithful church being the universal body of believers, with faithful Jesus as the head of that body. One day, Jesus will come back from heaven and claim his beautiful bride. Revelation 19:7-9 describes how Jesus and the church look forward to being married together in heaven forever.

Unfortunately, the Israelites, as recorded in the Old Testament of the Bible, did not want to be faithful to God. There were so many other tempting gods to worship. Baal worship was a favorite among God's people. God was still faithful and loving toward his unfaithful, idolatrous nation.

In an act of symbolism, God told the prophet Hosea to marry the prostitute Gomer. This unlikely union painted a living picture of both God's disgust for idolatry and his love for Israel. When Gomer became unfaithful to Hosea, God made another request. Hosea was to reunite with Gomer and show love to his unfaithful wife.

Gomer represents unfaithful Israel, who is married to a faithful, forgiving husband, Jesus. God loathes the sin of people because of holiness and justice; however, Jesus redeems sinful people by merciful grace. From eternity, Jesus planned to die in the place of his unfaithful bride.

Hanameel

Leviticus {25:25} If thy brother be waxen poor, and hath sold away [some] of his possession, and if any of his kin come to redeem it, then shall he redeem that which his brother sold.

THE LORD GIVETH AND THE LORD TAKETH AWAY IS A familiar phrase used when one experiences a great loss after enjoying many blessings. God's people, Israel and Judah, experienced great blessings from God in their promised land for many generations. The promised land was said to be flowing with milk and honey, fertile, and beautiful.

Unfortunately, God's people betrayed God in the promised land and sold out to idol worship. As a punishment, God took away the promised land from Israel and gave it to the king of Babylon. Just before this was to occur, God required Jeremiah to perform an act of symbolism documenting God's love for the chosen nation of Israel. God promised that one day he would restore Israel to their promised land.

Jeremiah {32:7} Behold, Hanameel the son of Shallum thine uncle shall come unto thee, saying, Buy thee my field that [is] in Anathoth: for the right of redemption [is] thine to buy [it.]

God's law allowed his people to redeem what was lost. The closest family relative, called a kinsman redeemer, would have the right to purchase the land back to keep it in the family. Like Hanameel sought the prophet Jeremiah to be a kinsman redeemer, Jesus seeks believers, as our closest family relative, for redemption to God.

The Brasen Altar

Hebrews {9:22} And almost all things are by the law purged with blood; and without shedding of blood is no remission.

GOD CHOSE KING SOLOMON TO BUILD THE TEMPLE WHERE God would dwell with the nation of Israel in Jerusalem. At the temple dedication, Solomon glorified God, lifting the people to God in prayer at the beginning of the time for burnt offerings and sacrifices. Solomon pleaded for God to hear the prayers of the people when they sin, have trouble with their neighbor or other nations, or if God should punish them with famine. Solomon even encouraged foreigners to pray to God.

God heard Solomon's prayer and sent fire from heaven to consume the sacrifices on the brasen altar. God used the brasen altar to make the offerings holy and shekinah glory filled the temple.

2 Chronicles {7:7} Moreover Solomon hallowed the middle of the court that [was] before the house of the LORD: for there he offered burnt offerings, and the fat of the peace offerings, because the brasen altar which Solomon had made was not able to receive the burnt offerings, and the meat offerings, and the fat.

No brasen altar is massive enough to receive a sacrifice worthy of God's holiness. The brasen altar was the place to make temporary sacrifices holy. Jesus's permanent altar of the cross was the place to make God's holy Son to become sin. God's faithful believers are now filled by the Holy Spirit's glory because Jesus's sacrifice was worthy of God's holiness.

Abraham

Genesis {12:1} Now the LORD had said unto Abram, Get thee out of thy country, and from thy kindred, and from thy father's house, unto a land that I will shew thee: {12:2} And I will make of thee a great nation, and I will bless thee, and make thy name great; and thou shalt be a blessing.

ASIDE FROM THE PROMISE FOUND IN GENESIS 3:15 THAT God would send a savior to lost humanity, sad news prevailed. First the fall in Eden, then the murder of Abel, next the catastrophic flood, followed by confusion at Babel. At last, in Genesis 12, good news—God provided another promise. A man named Abram, later renamed Abraham, trusted a wonderful promise from God.

God promised Abraham that he would be a source of blessing for all the nations in the earth. God invited Abraham to leave his home, his identity, his security, his land, and go to a place that he did not know. Abraham obeyed and trusted that God would do as promised. God would establish a new hope for humanity through Abraham. When Abraham was one hundred years old, his wife Sarah bore him a son named Isaac, the lineage of Jesus.

Abraham's family was the tiny family that grew into the great nation of Israel. Israel trusted God with great hope for their promised redeemer. God's covenant with Abraham included innumerable descendants and a tremendous territory of land. God used the land to grant Israel prosperity, to judge Israel, and this promised land would become the birthplace of Jesus.

Publius

Acts {28:7} In the same quarters were possessions of the chief man of the island, whose name was Publius; who received us, and lodged us three days courteously. {28:8} And it came to pass, that the father of Publius lay sick of a fever and of a bloody flux: to whom Paul entered in, and prayed, and laid his hands on him, and healed him. {28:9} So when this was done, others also, which had diseases in the island, came, and were healed.

THE JEWISH LEADERS SOUGHT TO KILL PAUL FOR TEACHING about Jesus and the resurrection. Roman authorities protected Paul by placing him into their custody as their prisoner. The Lord told Paul that he must testify before Caesar, so he boarded a ship as a prisoner headed to Rome.

During one sailing, a terrible storm put them in danger. Paul advised the prisoner guard that an angel visited him and advised that all the lives on the boat would be safe; however, the boat would be destroyed. Miraculously, all the people were brought safely to the island of Malta.

The people of Malta were amazed when a viper fastened on Paul's hand and Paul did not die.

Publius was the name given to chief men of the island. As the chief man, Publius trusted Paul. The natives of Malta also trusted Paul, and they received God's blessing of healing. Publius helped Paul declare the gospel of Jesus to the natives in Malta while on his way to Rome.

Egypt

Romans {5:9} Much more then, being now justified by his blood, we shall be saved from wrath through him.

GOD USED EGYPT AS A COVERING FROM FAMINE FOR ISRAEL where God's chosen family of seventy people grew to a nation of millions. The book of Exodus reveals how one Pharaoh did not remember why the Israelites were in Egypt, so he harshly oppressed them for their size, and ordered murder for their infant sons.

Not even Pharaoh's own daughter would murder a Hebrew baby, especially the one she saw floating in the Nile near the place where she would bathe. Moses's sister Miriam planned for the care of baby Moses until he was adopted into Egyptian royalty. As a man, Moses fled Egypt in fear for his life after murdering an Egyptian for harsh treatment of a Hebrew slave.

God directed Moses back to Egypt with power to free the Israelites. God sent many plagues against Egypt, and times of hardening Pharaoh's heart; however, one miraculous event resulted in setting the Hebrews free. God required his people to paint their doorposts with the blood of an unblemished lamb, sacrificed to cover and save the life of the first-born inside.

The angel of death passed over Egypt and killed all the first-born in every home, except for those who were covered under blood. This annual memorial is the Feast of the Passover.

Many centuries later, Egypt protected baby Jesus. Jesus's precious blood is like the covering of the Passover lamb in Egypt. Believers bypass eternal death and receive eternal life in Jesus's name.

Moses

*John {1:17} For the law was given by Moses, [but] grace
and truth came by Jesus Christ.*

WITHOUT LAWS, THERE CAN BE NO CIVILIZATION. LAWS
exist because of sin. Although laws vary from nation to nation,
they exist everywhere around the world.
God used the Levite Moses to lead the great tribe of
Israel from slavery in Egypt. God wanted fellowship with his
people; however, the sinful nature of humanity was a barrier.
To make the people clean, God established the Levitical law
on Mount Sinai.

God had Moses tell the people to obey God's laws and
be set apart for righteousness from the other nations for
God's glory. If the Israelites disobeyed God's laws, then judgment would follow. The covenant law was a legal agreement
between God and the chosen nation of Israel.

Jesus promised from eternity to cure the sinful helpless-
ness of humanity by his life of obedience to God's holy law.
The old covenant of obedience to the law is defeating for sinners; however, the new covenant of faith in Jesus is victory to
eternal life. Jesus obeyed the law given to Moses.

John Bunyan, author of *The Pilgrim's Progress* is often
credited with writing this fitting rhyme:

> *"Run, John, run, the law commands*
> *But gives neither feet nor hands,*
> *Far better news the gospel brings:*
> *It bids us fly and give us wings!"*

Vashti

Ephesians {5:24} Therefore as the church is subject unto Christ, so [let] the wives [be] to their own husbands in every thing. {5:25} Husbands, love your wives, even as Christ also loved the church, and gave himself for it.

THE BIBLICAL MODEL OF MARRIAGE EMBRACES THE ONENESS between one husband and one wife. Marriage is the depiction of the oneness that Christ has with his bride, the church. Marriages suffer when spouses are selfish and prideful. Scripture teaches that God does not want people to tear apart what God joined together because marriage is honorable and sacred.

The book of Esther details how Vashti's husband, King Ahasuerus, the king of Persia, gave a feast for the people of Susa. Queen Vashti also gave a banquet for all the women.

On the seventh day, the king ordered Vashti to bring her royal crown and reveal her beauty to all. Queen Vashti refused to obey this selfish request and the marriage ended.

Scripture helps married and unmarried people to have healthy relationships. Jesus is better than any earthly spouse because he always provides, he always listens, he always cares, he is always available, and he will never hurt or forsake us.

Vashti did not have a perfect king husband; however, God's faithful do have a perfect, loving husband in King Jesus. May the bride of Christ be bound to Jesus, whose love endures forever.

Chapter 2

Isaiah
{65:17} For, behold,
I create new
heavens and a new earth:
and the former
shall not be remembered,
nor come into mind.

The Woman of Samaria

John {4:9} Then saith the woman of Samaria unto him, How is it that thou, being a Jew, askest drink of me, which am a woman of Samaria? for the Jews have no dealings with the Samaritans. {4:10} Jesus answered and said unto her, If thou knewest the gift of God, and who it is that saith to thee, Give me to drink; thou wouldest have asked of him, and he would have given thee living water.

DRAWING WATER AT JACOB'S WELL WAS A HIGH POINT IN the day for most Samaritan women. Most women would socialize around the well during the cooler hours of the day. The woman of Samaria drew water alone during the heat of the day because she was an outcast by her people.

Jews traveled around Samaria to avoid the Samaritans. Jesus traveled through Samaria with the intent to meet the woman of Samaria for a divine conversation.

The woman of Samaria was spiritually impoverished, yet Jesus loved her enough to tell her about living water that springs up to eternal life. The woman of Samaria told people in her town of her encounter with the man who told her everything about her life.

Jesus is the Messiah sent from God to wash away sin with living water. Jesus loves sinners, and no one is beyond the love of God. The Holy Spirit fills hearts with a well spring of living water, welling to eternal life.

Melchisedec

Hebrews {7:15} And it is yet far more evident: for that after the similitude of Melchisedec there ariseth another priest, {7:16} Who is made, not after the law of a carnal commandment, but after the power of an endless life. {7:17} For he testifieth, Thou [art] a priest for ever after the order of Melchisedec.

THE ROLE OF THE PRIEST IS TO BRING GOD AND PEOPLE together in peace. Abraham met the priest Melchisedec upon return from battle. Abraham knew that Melchisedec's priesthood was superior to himself and his descendants, so he honored Melchisedec by giving him a tenth of all his wealth. Abraham's son Levi's descendants were God's chosen to serve God in the temple as priests.

The priesthood foreshadowed Jesus Christ as our great high priest who brings God and people together in righteousness. Annually on the "Day of Atonement," the high priest entered behind the temple curtain, into "the holy of holies" to make sacrifices as an atonement for sin.

The temple curtain that guarded the "holy of holies" miraculously tore in two as Jesus died on the cross. Jesus's sacrifice eliminated the need for temple sacrifice, so the "holy of holies" is open for all who receive faith in Jesus. Jesus brings God and people together as our high priest.

The Mosaic law is unable to permanently make atonement for sin due to the sinfulness of humankind and the temporary nature of the Levitical priesthood. God provided a better priesthood in Jesus. Like Melchisedec, Jesus Christ is not a descendant from the Levitical priesthood. Jesus's resurrection from the dead specifies a perfect priesthood to last forever.

Naaman

*2 Kings {5:14} Then went he down, and dipped himself
seven times in Jordan, according to the saying of the
man of God: and his flesh came again like unto the
flesh of a little child, and he was clean.*

THE BIBLE REVEALS THAT LEPROSY WAS A COMMON SKIN
disease that produced marring sores.

Naaman was a man with a healthy ego, whose master considered him a great man of valor because he was victorious in battle; however, he was a leper, and leprosy was defaming. Naaman's wife's servant girl knew of a prophet of God who could cure Naaman of his leprosy.

Naaman received permission from the king of Syria to go to the prophet for healing. When the prophet Elisha learned of Naaman's arrival he gave an unusual command. Wash seven times in the Jordan River. Naaman became offended, thinking the prophet should come heal him personally. Naaman's men persuaded him to go to the river to be clean.

Naaman received cleansing from the God of Israel in an unusual manner. Similarly, followers of Jesus set aside their healthy ego to trust exclusively in the precious blood that was shed at the cross of Christ for the forgiveness of sins.

God's splendor is often revealed in insignificant, obedient tasks. Leprosy is terrible but not as terrible as the sin condition. May believers set aside their ego and receive the free gift of simple faith in Jesus who died and rose again as our righteous substitute for the forgiveness of sins.

Nehemiah

*Proverbs {15:31} The ear that heareth the reproof
of life abideth among the wise.*

A PERSISTENT HABIT OF NEGLECTING TO READ AND UNDERSTAND
the Holy Bible will surely lead a believer toward spiritual decline.
Nehemiah was a cup bearer for King Artaxerxes. The king
honored Nehemiah's request to go to Jerusalem to rebuild the
walls and gates around the city after the Babylonian capture. The
temple was destroyed and the city burned. Nehemiah arrived with
official documents to gain access to necessary materials.

God provided people to work, as well as protection from
enemies. Nehemiah provided for the workers, stopped oppressive
practices, and participated in a celebration, where he read the law
clearly for the people to understand. The Jews committed their
lives to the Lord, vowing to follow the laws of Moses.

Nehemiah resumed his role as cupbearer to the king. In time
he learned that the Jews fell back into their sinful patterns, neglecting the Sabbath and intermarrying with the idolatrous people.

Upon Nehemiah's return to Jerusalem, he disciplined the
Jews harshly for their spiritual decline, and prayed for them.
Nehemiah's best work was strengthening the hearts of God's
people to be spiritually inclined to follow God's laws.

Like Nehemiah, Jesus strengthens the hearts of God's
people and protects them from the enemy. Jesus sees rebellion in God's people, so he too must discipline them. Jesus
sends believers the Holy Spirit who helps the faithful to clearly
understand the Bible and he convicts them of sin. Jesus also
prays for God's faithful, and he desires our obedience. May
we be faithful to Jesus.

Hezekiah

2 Kings {19:35} And it came to pass that night, that the angel of the LORD went out, and smote in the camp of the Assyrians an hundred fourscore and five thousand: and when they arose early in the morning, behold, they [were] all dead corpses.

SOME PEOPLE TALK A BIG TALK; HOWEVER, THEY DO NOT live by their words. Others are faithful in both word and deed; they talk the talk and they walk the walk.

Hezekiah became king of Judah at age twenty-five. Immediately, King Hezekiah set out to restore Judah, and all of Israel, to set their hearts toward the Lord. Hezekiah talked the talk, and he walked the walk by removing idolatry, by restoring the Passover Feast, and by praying to God.

As a faithful king, Hezekiah prayed for the Jews who were not ceremonially clean during their feast, and God healed them. Hezekiah prayed for God's mercy for his own life when he was sick and dying, and God's healing extended his life.

One time, Hezekiah made a desperate prayer for deliverance from the king of Assyria who was a great threat to the chosen nation of Israel. Hezekiah prayed for victory over the Assyrians and God fought for his people by sending the angel of the Lord to smite the Assyrian camp.

Like Hezekiah, Jesus knows the power of prayer. Do not underestimate the power of prayer in Jesus's name. Jesus walked the walk, talked the talk, and prays the church to victory.

Zerubbabel

Haggai {2:4} Yet now be strong, O Zerubbabel, saith the LORD; and be strong, O Joshua, son of Josedech, the high priest; and be strong, all ye people of the land, saith the LORD, and work: for [I am] with you, saith the LORD of hosts:

CONTRARY TO THE OLD SAYING, "WHEN GOD CLOSES A door, he opens a window," God may will to close a door and lock the window. God's people turned away from God and worshiped idols in the majestic temple built by King Solomon, so God closed that door. Enemies destroyed the beautiful temple and God locked the window for a time.

In time, God appointed Zerubbabel, governor of Judah, to lead the temple restoration. As the Israelites worked, their noise was indistinct, a combination of immense joy and laments of grief.

The young were joyous because the temple was to be restored. The old who were familiar with Solomon's beautiful temple were grievous for the lackluster of the renovation.

Mankind disobeyed God in the garden of Eden, so God closed the door for fellowship. God did not open a window for sinful humans, he opened another majestic door for free fellowship.

Zerubbabel led Israel's temple restoration. Jesus led the temple restoration for sinful human hearts. Jesus is the door to life for the house of God because of the cross and the regenerating, restoring, and renovating power of the Spirit.

Zaccheus

Luke {19:5} And when Jesus came to the place, he looked up, and saw him, and said unto him, Zaccheus, make haste, and come down; for today I must abide at thy house.

WHEN SOMEONE HAS BOTH GOOD NEWS AND SAD NEWS TO share, they usually like to share the sad news first. This way there is hope for the hearer to be glad for the good news to follow.

Scripture teaches that it is impossible for a rich person to find their way into heaven; this is sad news for the rich. The good news is that what is impossible for man is possible with God.

Zaccheus was starstruck by Jesus. Due to Zaccheus's small stature, he climbed into a tall tree to see Jesus walk by. Zaccheus was a Jew who collected taxes on his fellow Jews on behalf of the Roman government, and likely he extorted extra money for himself.

Jesus exonerated Zaccheus and called him a child of Abraham due to his genuine faith that led to action, not by his lineage. Zaccheus offered to refund any fraudulent charges, by fourfold.

The sad news is that sinners do not deserve forgiveness of sins. The good news is that Jesus Christ offers the opportunity to repent of our sins, so that we may receive a new heart for the cultivation of good works here on earth and eternal life in his name.

Martha

Luke {10:41} And Jesus answered and said unto her, Martha, Martha, thou art careful and troubled about many things: {10:42} But one thing is needful: and Mary hath chosen that good part, which shall not be taken away from her.

IF GOD GIVES YOU A SIBLING WHO LOVES YOU, FORGIVES you, and will help you despite your differences, you have a good thing. Such was the case for the friends of Jesus, Mary, and Martha.

These loving sisters welcomed Jesus into their hearts and home with gladness, and Martha began preparations for a feast. Martha's sister Mary chose to sit and listen at the feet of Jesus while Martha worked. Martha lost her patience with Mary and asked Jesus to advise her sister to help.

Martha's sister recognized the sweeter tasting portion and sat at Jesus's feet. Listening to spiritual words spoken from the Lord, in a family home, must have been all-consuming to Mary.

Martha meant well; she was preparing a feast. Anyone familiar with a banquet would understand the immense level of effort required. How fortunate for Mary that Jesus understood her need for spiritual food and allowed her to remain.

Martha was eager to serve Jesus; however, she became distracted by the service and temporarily lost sight of the precious one to serve. Jesus calls the faithful to serve the church well, and the work is hard. May we avoid distraction from the precious one we serve, the Lord Jesus Christ.

King Uzziah

Isaiah {6:1} In the year that king Uzziah died I saw also the Lord sitting upon a throne, high and lifted up, and his train filled the temple.

A DIFFICULT THING TO WITNESS IS A WELL-RESPECTED person in authority losing their position because of a deliberate, disgraceful deed. It is sad when a rich life ends poorly. King Uzziah ruled as a good king in Judah, from the age of sixteen, for fifty-two years in peace and prosperity. Uzziah's reputation for being a great military leader, an inventor, a gifted intellectual, a builder of land, and his love for holy God made him famous in the ancient world.

Unfortunately, pride took root in the king's heart. King Uzziah disgraced himself by deliberately attempting to burn incense to the Lord in the temple. The priests tried to stop the angry king.

God punished King Uzziah with leprosy. The king lived and died apart from his people and he was buried without honor. With the death of King Uzziah, Israel's national prosperity ended. The prophet Isaiah began to prophesy of Israel's pending destruction and certain Babylonian captivity, as a judgment for the deliberate, disgraceful deeds of the people.

With the death of King Jesus, human captivity to sin ended. The Holy Spirit offers hope for sinners to avoid deliberate, disgraceful destruction as a judgment for sin. Jesus's life, death, and resurrection allow humans to not end poorly. Jesus gives the faithful forgiveness of sins and eternal life in his name.

The Cripple

Acts {14:8} And there sat a certain man at Lystra,
impotent in his feet, being a cripple from his mother's
womb, who never had walked.

THERE WAS NO TEMPLE FOR THE LORD IN LYSTRA AND THE Gentiles only knew of idol worship. By the power of the Holy Spirit, the Lycaonians witnessed Paul and Barnabas heal a faithful cripple.

The people at Lystra did not know any better, so they tried to offer sacrifices to Paul and Barnabas. Paul and Barnabas begged the people to not worship them. New believers have a lot to learn about how to worship the Lord Jesus.

The Bible clearly reveals God's will for people to forsake idolatry and focus on the person and work of Jesus exclusively. The God who created the world and sent a holy Savior demands an exclusive commitment to worship in spirit and in truth. Believers may not serve God alongside their own idols because God desires all the glory.

Many do not grasp that praying to statues, deceased people, objects, and consecrated images are all ways of stealing God's glory and giving his glory to objects. Finding comfort in any material things is a form of idol worship when these things are desired more than desiring God.

When a person becomes a believer in the Lord Jesus it is important for them to learn how to worship God and avoid idol worship. Idolatry is a serious, sinful offense to God. God wants believers to worship Jesus in spirit and in truth in accordance with the scriptures.

Caesarea Philippi

Matthew {16:13} When Jesus came into the coasts of Caesarea Philippi, he asked his disciples, saying, Whom do men say that I the Son of man am?

SIMON PETER ANSWERED THAT JESUS IS THE MESSIAH. Only God reveals truth to believers. Caesarea Philippi was the center of idol worship with the gods Baal, Pan, and Caesar being central to the region. Jesus and the disciples were surrounded with idols, rituals, and false hope of pleasing a non-existent deity.

Acts {17:23} For as I passed by, and beheld your devotions, I found an altar with this inscription, TO THE UNKNOWN GOD. Whom therefore ye ignorantly worship.

Polytheism, the worship of many gods; atheism, the worship of no God; and pantheism, the infinite but impersonal god, all pale in comparison to the God of the Bible. The God of the Bible is a personal, self-existent, eternal, and sovereign God who distinctively identifies in three ways: God the Father, God the Son, and God the Holy Spirit. God is the "I AM," the creator of the universe, the law giver, the just judge, and the justifier.

Believers live in a world like Caesarea Philippi because there are idols everywhere. People will either worship a God who demands holiness or they will worship a god that they can mold into their lifestyle.

Those with faith in Jesus will be reconciled to God and will dwell with him forever. Those without faith in Jesus will be separated from the God of the Bible and will dwell away from him forever. Who do you think Jesus is?

Ananias

*Acts {9:17} And Ananias went his way, and entered
into the house; and putting his hands on him said,
Brother Saul, the Lord, [even] Jesus, that appeared
unto thee in the way as thou camest, hath sent me,
that thou mightest receive thy sight, and be filled
with the Holy Ghost.*

DISCIPLES OF THE LORD ARE OFTEN PLACED IN UNCOM-
fortable circumstances to accomplish God's will. Believers
decide many details in life; however, the Lord is the one
directing the stride. Believers can trust that every life detail
is in God's hands even if we do not quite understand.

Ananias was a highly respected observer of the law who
received a frightening, worrisome directive from the Lord.
Ananias was to cure the blindness of Saul of Tarsus, a Roman-
Jew, who approved of the murder of Christians.

After praying for clarity, Ananias trusted and obeyed the
Lord's leading and found Saul. Ananias cured Saul's blindness, and Saul understood truth in scriptures concerning
the person and work of Jesus. Saul received a new name, the
Apostle Paul, author of much of the New Testament.

Facing uncomfortable circumstances to do God's will
requires trust and obedience. Ananias reminds that following
God's plan may feel uncomfortable, so trust and obey, and
find direction by prayer in Jesus's name. It is not up to the
believer to overcome obstacles, to win battles, or to accomplish personal goals; it is up to the believer to yield to the
leading of the Holy Spirit.

Hushai

2 Samuel {17:7} And Hushai said unto Absalom, The counsel that Ahithophel hath given [is] not good at this time.

THERE IS AN OLD SAYING: "TWO HEADS ARE BETTER THAN one," so seeking counsel is wise. Solving big problems requires trusted, wise counsel. Defining the problem, goal setting, considering options, picking a strategy, execution, and evaluation are all necessary steps for problem-solving success.

Hushai was a friend to King David. Absalom was planning to kill David and take over his kingdom and needed trusted counsel. Absalom received counsel from a wise source by the name of Ahithophel. Absalom wanted to hear if Hushai agreed with Ahithophel's advice for him to select twelve thousand soldiers to overtake his tired father. Hushai was Absalom's enemy.

King David's friend Hushai did not have Absalom's best interest at heart. Hushai advised on Absalom's problem of his father and the goal to murder him. God used Hushai's prudent speech and convincing similes to evaluate an option that played on the vanity of Absalom. Absalom's pride was enticed to pick the strategy that would execute the delay of attack and abandon Ahithophel's counsel. Absalom's delay allowed Hushai to direct word back that David had time to escape. Absalom trusted the wrong source and he died.

Through Hushai, God showed mercy to King David and rescued him from death. Through Jesus, God shows mercy to sinners and rescues them from death when they trust him. Sin is a big problem that requires wise counsel, so do not trust the enemy. Only trust in Jesus for eternal life.

Nabal

James {3:5} Even so the tongue is a little member, and boasteth great things. Behold, how great a matter a little fire kindleth!

EVERYONE IS GUILTY AT ONE TIME OR ANOTHER OF USING our communication to stir the pot. No one wants to admit enjoying causing trouble for others; however, far too many of us have. Whether it be a sibling rivalry, or a peer or spousal conflict, all benefit from a controlled tongue.

The book of 1 Samuel describes Nabal as a worthless man who lacked discretion. King Saul sought to kill David, so David took shelter in the wilderness. Nabal's servants enjoyed protection from David and his men as they kept sheep and prepared for Nabal's feast.

David hoped to join Nabal's feast; however, upon request Nabal evilly rebuked David's men, dishonoring them and sending them away. Upon learning of the rejection David was determined to murder Nabal's household. Nabal's servants had no choice but to beg Nabal's wife for help. Nabal's wife intervened and saved innocent lives.

Nabal reminds that people are sinners who need prayer to tame the tongue. Thankfully, Jesus lives to make intercession for believers at the throne of God and prays that followers use words that bring God glory.

Sometimes the tiniest word can cause enormous effect. Learn to be strategic with word choices because it can have influence when it comes to life-or-death issues. May we use our speech to share the gospel of Christ with love.

Chapter 3

Jeremiah
{18:6} O house of Israel,
cannot I do with you
as this potter?
saith the LORD.
Behold, as the clay [is] in
the potter's hand,
so [are] ye in mine hand,
O house of Israel.

Abigail

Proverbs {25:11} A word fitly spoken [is like] apples of gold in pictures of silver.

FINE JEWELRY IS A DESIRABLE FORM OF BEAUTY TO ADORN the wearer. Fine jewelry can send a message about our character. Having Godly speech can also be like wearing a beautiful ornament. The opposite of a gracious speaker would be the volatile. Such was the contrast in the couple of Abigail and Nabal in 1 Samuel. Abigail had a beautiful character; Nabal, was worthless.

David was the anointed future heir to the throne of Israel, and his men were in the wilderness of Paran, because King Saul sought to kill David. A large banquet was being prepared and numerous sheep were being sheared. David respectfully sent ten of his men to Nabal to request that David and his men join in on the feast, as they were helpful and protected Nabal's shepherds. Upon arrival, Nabal was insolent to the men and sent them back with grave insult. David immediately vowed to murder Nabal's entire household.

Upon this discovery, Abigail quickly acted. Without telling Nabal, Abigail saddled a donkey, and she brought the men a feast. Abigail offered atonement for her sinful husband and David gave her a blessing. When Nabal learned of his offense, his heart failed and he died; David made Abigail his wife.

Jesus pleads for the atonement of sinners like Abigail pleaded for forgiveness. May hearts be filled by the gracious, beautiful character of the Holy Spirit, the finest ornament for the human soul.

Eutychus

Acts {20:9} And there sat in a window a certain young man named Eutychus, being fallen into a deep sleep: and as Paul was long preaching, he sunk down with sleep, and fell down from the third loft, and was taken up dead.

EUTYCHUS IS DESCRIBED AS A YOUNG ADULT; LISTENING to Paul's speech about the Lord Jesus. As they were breaking bread together, likely after a long day, the speech went on and on, until it was very late. Some who are familiar with young adults will agree that when they are tired out, they will find it hard to stay awake.

One can only imagine the terror and grief the adults in this young man's life must have felt. No doubt they were comforted immensely when Paul scooped the young man up and brought him back from the dead. Eutychus's experience as a young adult was a miraculous gift from God.

One of the best things an adult can do for a young adult is accompany them in church regularly. Belonging to a local fellowship of believers where there is ongoing speech of Jesus and breaking bread is a great way to honor the Lord. In the church setting, you can make friends, a positive difference, serve the Lord, pray, help to hold each other accountable, participate in social events, and bring children and young adults to learn about Jesus. The youth are the future of the church.

Saul of Tarsus

*Acts {9:4} And he fell to the earth, and heard a voice
saying unto him, Saul, Saul, why persecutest thou me?*

EVERY PERSON MUST ALIGN WITH GOD'S LOVING PLAN OF
redemption through the person and work of the Lord Jesus
Christ, or they will remain in spiritual darkness for all eternity.
Those who reject Jesus as Lord tend to harbor various feelings
of resentment for Christians who believe in the righteousness of Jesus. Nonbelievers either feel that they are righteous
enough on their own without God, or they feel that a righteous God would never accept or forgive them as they are.

Before the Apostle Paul became a servant of Jesus, he was
known as Saul of Tarsus. Saul, a Roman Jew, hated Christians.
Saul thought it foolish that the Messiah would be bodily
resurrected from the grave in the form of a righteous man
to judge the earth and rule forever as Lord. Saul harbored so
much hatred that he imprisoned and approved of the murder
of Christians. On one occasion, as Saul was on a murderous
journey, a miracle happened.

Jesus addressed Saul and caused him to be blind until
Ananias would come to heal his sight. God cured Saul's
spiritual blindness and equipped him with knowledge and
power to preach God's plan of salvation. Later renamed
Paul, Saul became one of the most important missionaries
in the world, he suffered for the gospel, and wrote much of
the New Testament.

Eli

Proverbs {13:24} He that spareth his rod hateth his son: but he that loveth him chasteneth him betimes.

PARENTING IS ONE OF THE MORE DEBATED TOPICS AROUND. What do you do with a wayward child? God's priest Eli lacked disciplinary parenting for his sons Hophni and Phineas.

The Levite livelihood depended on their role as priest. Eli's failure to put God's will before the will of his sons resulted in a curse from God.

1 Samuel {2:34} And this [shall be] a sign unto thee, that shall come upon thy two sons, on Hophni and Phinehas; in one day they shall die both of them.

The Israelites were nearby their Philistine enemies and were making a loud noise. The ark of the covenant, which contained God's treasures and the ten commandments, was with the Israelites. The Philistines attacked and captured the ark.

When Eli heard men returning from battle, he was trembling. Eli was ninety-eight years old and heavy set. When Eli learned of the capture of the ark of God and the death of both of his sons, he fell out of his seat backward, broke his neck, and died.

Jesus's faithful believers are adopted into the family of God, and with that comes discipline. Discipline from Father God is painful. Eli was not willing to cause his sons pain, as a result they died. Jesus cares enough to discipline the children of God, even if it hurts, because the discipline of the Lord benefits the faithful in matters of eternal life.

Micah

Micah {6:8} He hath shewed thee, O man, what [is] good;
and what doth the LORD require of thee, but to do justly,
and to love mercy, and to walk humbly with thy God?

GOD SENT PROPHETS TO WARN THE PEOPLE OF IMMINENT
danger. During a time, when the Israelites were constantly
sinful, God sent them the prophet Micah. Micah explained
their sin, announced their punishment, and proclaimed their
eventual restoration. Warnings should be heeded.

Micah exposed God's will for his people in the concept
of threes. God desires his people to do what is right, to show
compassion, and resist pride. The gospel reveals the perfect
set of three: rebellion, repentance, and reconciliation. God's
Word warns that sinful rebellion separates people from God
forever. Sinners are invited to repent of their sin in Jesus's
name, so to be reconciled to God in righteousness forever.
When believers respond to the perfect three—rebellion,
repentance, and reconciliation—then their gift of faith offers
security of the inheritance of eternal life. Repentant people
are sinners who avoid sin and follow Jesus in the power of
the Holy Spirit. Regretfully, people will commit and confess
sin until they are glorified with Jesus in heaven.

To do justice, to love kindness, and to walk humbly with
God are the three perfect forms of love. The cross serves as a
warning sign to sinners of their choice between eternal death
and eternal life. Victory to eternal life comes by faith in Jesus's
finished work on the cross.

The Fourth Man

Daniel {3:25} He answered and said, Lo, I see four men loose, walking in the midst of the fire, and they have no hurt; and the form of the fourth is like the Son of God.

REJECTION AND PERSECUTION FOR NONCONFORMITY HAVE been commonplace since ancient times. Individuals who commit to an ideology tend to become exclusive and prejudiced. When powerful individuals use their power to force their system into exclusivity, many will perish.

King Nebuchadnezzar of Babylon was enormously powerful, so he decided to create a massive image of gold, tall enough for the entire region to see. The king commanded that there would be a call to worship, and every person would bow down and worship the golden image or else be thrown into a fiery furnace. Three young men offended Nebuchadnezzar by refusing to worship the image, regardless of whether their powerful God would rescue them from the fiery furnace.

Jesus walked in the fire, as the fourth man in the fiery furnace, with the appearance of the Son of God. The three men, Shadrach, Meshack, and Abednego, did not have a hint of smoke on them when they came out of the fiery furnace. Jesus identifies with the persecuted church and walks with believers during the heated times of trial that refine them like pure silver and gold.

Each day offers the opportunity for God's faithful to be brave and trust God. Society pressures believers to conform to worldview ideology that is not in accordance with the Bible. Believers will walk through heated trials with Jesus at our side.

The Altar of Incense

Exodus {30:5} And thou shalt make the staves [of]
shittim wood, and overlay them with gold. {30:6} And
thou shalt put it before the vail that [is] by the ark of
the testimony, before the mercy seat that [is] over the
testimony, where I will meet with thee.

NEWER BELIEVERS MAY FIND THAT THEY STRUGGLE WITH
prayer, especially corporate prayer. Praying in agreement with
others brings God glory as the saints are gathered as one body.
God created believers for fellowship. Prayer brings God glory
as observed in the altar of incense.

The fragrant aroma of incense every morning and evening,
brought by the priests on behalf of the people with a right
heart, is something holy to God. The altar of incense was set
in front of the veil, apart from the holy of holies. At the cross,
Jesus's shed blood made the earth quake and the veil of the
temple was torn in two. Now, fragrant prayer in the name of
Jesus, from hearts go directly to God, and God meets with
them wherever they are.

The altar of incense reminds us that God desires to meet
us when we pray for God's will in Jesus's name. Morning
prayer allows for worship and consecration to God. After-
noon prayers may offer thanksgiving and intercessory prayers
for others. At evening prayers of supplication often flow
asking God to help in areas of struggle. Some wake up during
the night asking God for judgment or have prayers for healing.
How will you be praying today?

Felix

*Acts {24:25} And as he reasoned of righteousness,
temperance, and judgment to come Felix trembled,
and answered, Go thy way for this time; when I have
a convenient season, I will call for thee.*

SPIRITUAL PROCRASTINATION IS A TRAP THAT MANY PEOPLE
fall into. Many are on the fence concerning faith and waiting
for a better time to commit. Felix was intrigued by the followers of Jesus and had an opportunity to get to know the Apostle
Paul. Governor Felix had the privilege of personal meetings
with Paul as often as he wanted, as Paul was being detained in
custody for living out his faith and for telling others about Jesus.

Scripture does not reveal if Felix confessed a saving faith
in Jesus; however, his conscience was bothered by Paul's teaching. There is significant risk in spiritual procrastination. No
one knows when Jesus will return. Felix put off Jesus, risking
a harder heart for any future opportunity.

In Matthew 25:1-13, Jesus told a parable regarding heaven.
Ten virgins were invited to a wedding; however, they did not
know when the bridegroom would come for them. After a
while they slept, when in the night the bridegroom arrived.
Five of the virgins were prepared with oil for their lamps,
and the other five were not. The unprepared virgins were left
behind and the door was closed to them.

Spiritual procrastination, either by neglecting to share the
gospel or by delaying accepting the gospel is serious. May Jesus's
followers be persistent and deliberate in receiving and sharing
the gospel of forgiveness of sins and eternal life in Jesus's name.

The King of Ai

*Deuteronomy {11:26} Behold, I set before you this day
a blessing and a curse; {11:27} A blessing, if ye obey
the commandments of the LORD your God, which I
command you this day: {11:28} And a curse, if ye will
not obey the commandments of the LORD.*

WHEN A VICTORY IS EXPERIENCED, THERE IS USUALLY A
feeling of superiority that does not disappear quickly; however, some losses are so surprising that a rematch is required.

In the book of Joshua God gave the Israelites victory over
Jericho, but sin in the camp made God withhold victory over
Ai. God's people were unable to be victorious without God
fighting on their behalf. God wishes to bless those who love
him and keep his commands.

After the sin in the camp was removed, God revealed a
rematch. Israel ambushed Ai from behind while Joshua and
his men feigned defeat. The king of Ai was lured away in pur-
suit of what he thought was the Israelite army, meanwhile his
kingdom was burning at the hand of the Israelites. Ai's king
was murdered, and the Israelites claimed the victory over Ai
with God's help. The rematch set the record straight.

The king of Ai's short-lived victory reminds that there was
a time when God's enemy thought he was victorious. Satan
thought he won the battle for eternal human death when he
caused them to sin and be cursed. Thankfully, Jesus Christ
obeyed God's commands and obtained the blessing of eternal
life for all who believe in his victorious life. Jesus's rematch
set the record straight.

The Brass Serpent

John {3:14} And as Moses lifted up the serpent in the
wilderness, even so must the Son of man be lifted up:
{3:15} That whosoever believeth in him should not
perish, but have eternal life.

WHEN THE ISRAELITES FOLLOWED MOSES TO FREEDOM
from slavery in Egypt, they became discouraged. The food
was not as good as what they enjoyed in Egypt, and they began
to deride Moses for allowing the people to suffer. God's people
were discourteous to God and Moses.

God responded to their grumbling by sending fiery ser-
pents that bit the people, and many died. Moses prayed for the
people, so God told him to create an image of a fiery serpent
of brass and fix it on a pole. All who looked up to the brass
serpent in faith would receive healing.

God responded with grace to the repentant Israelites by
providing a way of healing through the channel of faith. The
brass serpent reminds how the cross of Jesus heals. Jesus was
lifted on the cross so that God could rightfully punish human
sin by taking the punishment upon himself.

When we experience tough times that make us grumble,
or are feeling happy and blessed, it is helpful to have verses
of scripture memorized for prayers of supplication, peace,
comfort, praise, and thanksgiving. God has no obligation to
tolerate sinful humanity, yet he loves sinners. Jesus chose to
be lifted on the cross to die, so that believers may be forgiven
and have eternal life.

Hagar

Genesis {16:13} And she called the name of the LORD
that spake unto her, Thou God seest me: for she said,
Have I also here looked after him that seeth me?

IT IS SO TEMPTING TO TAKE CIRCUMSTANCES INTO OUR
own hands when we see that life is not going according to our
plan. When heart knowledge and mind knowledge conflict,
we must trust God's wisdom and be content in his will.

God delayed giving children to Abraham and his wife,
Sarai. Later renamed Sarah, Abraham's wife trusted God's
promise that her husband's descendants would be too numerous to count. Sarah believed the promise in her heart; however,
in her mind she knew that she was too old.

It was culturally acceptable to alleviate the problem of
barrenness by the giving of a servant to the master of the
house to establish a family, so Sarah took circumstances into
her own hands. Sarah's handmaid Hagar bore Abraham a
son named Ishmael.

Years later, Sarah bore Abraham the son of the promise,
named Isaac. Isaac was the promised lineage to Jesus. Hagar
and her son were cast out of Abraham's home. God is omni-
present, everywhere all the time. God has many names, one
is "El Roi" meaning The God who sees. Hagar and Ishmael
were seen, blessed, and mercifully protected by loving God.

The son of the law, Ishmael, and the son of the promise,
Isaac, are both descendants of Abraham. Both are still con-
testing the promised land and their lineage to the Messiah.
Jesus saw Hagar.

The Man of God

1 Kings {13:14} And went after the man of God, and found him sitting under an oak: and he said unto him, [Art] thou the man of God that camest from Judah? And he said, I [am.]{13:15} Then he said unto him, Come home with me, and eat bread. {13:16} And he said, I may not return with thee, nor go in with thee: neither will I eat bread nor drink water with thee in this place: {13:17} For it was said to me by the word of the LORD.

DISOBEDIENCE OFTEN LEADS TO AN UNFORTUNATE END. When well-intended and beneficial instructions are issued from one who has the other's best interest at heart, the best result will come from discernment and obedience.

God sent a man to King Jeroboam to prophesy against the Israelites. The man of God had specific instruction from God for his journey. The man of God was to be discerning and obedient to God's will.

Instead, the man of God obeyed a lying prophet and ate with him. Regretfully, many people become distracted and disobey. The mistake of lacking discernment and disobedience cost the man of God his life and legacy, he was killed by a lion and buried in the lying prophet's tomb.

Jesus is discerning and obedient to God's will; he has the best interest at heart for the faithful. Jesus is not distracted and docs the will of the Father. Opportunity is offered daily for Jesus's followers to discern and obey or to disobey. Do you trust Jesus's will by your discernment and obedience?

The Sacrifice

Romans {5:1} Therefore being justified by faith, we have peace with God through our Lord Jesus Christ.

FIVE MAJOR SACRIFICIAL OFFERINGS WERE GIVEN SO GOD would have peace with his people. Sin disqualified peaceful fellowship with God, so God created a strategy for people to acquire a right heart. After specific ceremonial washings with water, God used the priests to offer the blood of unblemished animals on the altar to atone for sinful, guilty souls.

The *burnt offering* was to be unblemished male livestock and the priest laid hands on the head for the atonement of the sin of himself and the people. The burnt offering was for petitions to God and for praise to God's name, everything was burned on the altar, except skin. The *sin offering* and the *guilt offering* were individual offerings of similar fashion with some differences. These offerings provided atonement for committed sins, and they purged the guilt of conscience.

The *peace offering* was like the animal sacrifice; however, the desire was to have fellowship with the Lord and the offered meat was shared by the people who brought the sacrifice. The *grain offering* consisted of fine flour, frankincense, and oil, where the best was brought to the Lord, and some was burnt on the altar. Cooked or uncooked, this was a food offering to the Lord. The sacrifices provided some provision for the priests to eat, except for the burnt offering.

Believers rejoice that Jesus's sacrifice is enough, so no further sacrifice is required for the forgiveness of sin or guilt of conscience. Jesus made perfect atonement for sins at the cross.

Manoah

Isaiah {6:5} Then said I, Woe [is] me! for I am undone;
because I [am] a man of unclean lips, and I dwell in
the midst of a people of unclean lips: for mine eyes have
seen the King, the LORD of hosts.
Genesis {32:30} And Jacob called the name of the place Peniel:
for I have seen God face to face, and my life is preserved.
Judges {6:22} I have seen an angel of the LORD face to face.
{6:23} And the LORD said unto him, Peace [be] unto thee;
fear not: thou shalt not die.

ISAIAH, JACOB, AND GIDEON ALL HAD THE SAME FEAR AS
Manoah when they encountered God.

Manoah was a man of prayer during an evil time in Israel's
history. Manoah's wife was barren when the angel of the
Lord visited her and told her that she would conceive a son,
a Nazarite. Manoah's wife was to refrain from strong drink
and not to eat any unclean thing.

Manoah prayed for the angel to explain what they should
do with the promised child. The angel explained that Manoah's son, Samson, would be set apart from the Israelites, no
razor would touch his hair, and he would begin to save Israel
from the Philistines.

Judges {13:22} And Manoah said unto his wife, We shall
surely die, because we have seen God.

When Jesus returns to earth in Lordship, humanity will
experience the same fear that Manoah felt. Some will fear in
awe of God's holiness and others will fear God's wrath.

Chapter 4

John {1:29}
The next day John
seeth Jesus coming
unto him, and saith,
Behold the Lamb of God,
which taketh away
the sin of the world.

Eve

Genesis {3:15} And I will put enmity between thee and the woman, and between thy seed and her seed; it shall bruise thy head, and thou shalt bruise his heel.

HUMAN BEINGS ARE ALL MADE IN THE IMAGE OF GOD, from conception to eternity. Both males and females are of equal value. Women all experience pain during childbirth, and often, they desire to be equally as powerful as men.

Eve was the first woman made in the image of God, the first companion, and the first wife. Eve's name means "the living," because Eve was the first mother. During creation, God made the first person, Adam, out of dust from earth. When it was time to make Eve, she was made from Adam.

Genesis 2 reveals that Eve was made from the existing tissue that Adam was made of, demonstrating that both Adam and Eve were made of equal value. God used Adam's rib for the matter for creating woman, and women are rightfully to be by men's side in God's perfect plan for marriage and family.

Satan tempted Eve with fruit from God's forbidden tree in the garden of Eden. Eve offered the fruit to Adam who willfully ate in rebellion to God. Adam's sin brought about the curse of eternal death for all of humanity. The escape from eternal death was promised by God to come from the seed of the woman, from Eve. Eve was the conduit for the tempter for sin, and through Eve and womankind came the remedy for sin, the birth of Lord Jesus Christ.

Sinai

Galatians {4:21} Tell me, ye that desire to be under the law, do ye not hear the law? {4:22} For it is written, that Abraham had two sons, the one by a bondmaid, the other by a freewoman.

THROUGH GOD'S COVENANT WITH ABRAHAM, SCRIPTURE reveals God's will to love those whom he chooses to love. Through Sinai, scripture reveals God's law, character, and standard of holiness. Scripture reveals repeatedly that God's people are not able to follow the law perfectly, disqualifying them from standing righteously before holy God.

God chose Sinai to speak to Moses from a burning bush to reveal glory. On Sinai's holy ground, God commanded Moses to set the Israelites free from slavery in Egypt. At Sinai, God revealed his holiness to the Israelites by setting them apart from the other nations, holding them legally accountable to God's laws of righteousness.

God's faithful sin and are failures in their responsibility to the law, and the wage of sin is death. For this reason, Jesus chose to come from heaven to live perfectly as a holy man, so to die as a perfect man without sin, and be raised to a new life in righteousness.

Jesus died on the cross as our death substitute, so we may have freedom in his righteousness, and eternal life in his name. God must punish sinful humanity, so Jesus humbly accepted our penalty. The Holy Spirit testifies to our heart that we are qualified for heaven because Jesus set us free from our bond of obedience to Sinai's law.

MONDAY MORNING

Maher-shalal-hash-baz

Isaiah {8:1} Moreover the LORD said unto me,
Take thee a great roll, and write in it with a man's pen
concerning Maher-shalal-hash-baz.

SOMETIMES IT IS DIFFICULT TO DISCERN BETWEEN AN ALLY AND an enemy. Making decisions based on unreliable sources must be avoided because trusting the enemy can result in destruction.

The prophet Isaiah was giving King Ahaz of Judah the message from God concerning an enemy, who appeared to have the upper hand in a battle. Isaiah encouraged King Ahaz to trust the Lord, that God planned to give Judah the victory from the hand of his enemy. At the direction of God, Isaiah put the oath in writing that King Ahaz could trust his best ally, who was the Lord God.

God provided King Ahaz a written prophecy that Judah would be saved, and the wealth of Judah's enemies would be given to the king of Assyria before Isaiah's baby Maher-shalal-hash-baz would be old enough to speak the words "my father" or "my mother." Regretfully, King Ahaz trusted himself and made an agreement with the king of Assyria.

As God declared, Judah was saved; however, the unnecessary decision to ally with Assyria was a mistake. Assyria eventually destroyed Judah. Ahaz trusted in an enemy instead of trusting in God.

Maher-shalal-hash-baz was a child of promise, a promise that God is trustworthy. Jesus was born a child of promise too, a promise that God is trustworthy. Humans will either align with life in Jesus or death by the enemy. May we always decide to trust Jesus, our best ally for eternal life.

Mary

John {1:14} And the Word was made flesh, and dwelt among us, (and we beheld his glory, the glory as of the only begotten of the Father,) full of grace and truth.

IT IS IMPOSSIBLE FOR THE HUMAN MIND TO KNOW AND understand God completely. The Bible is our best resource for seeking wisdom and understanding. Apart from scripture, our search for spiritual knowledge should cease.

Out of God's great love, Mary was chosen to be the vessel to deliver baby Jesus into the world, for the sake of grace and mercy for humanity. Grace is blessing received from God without merit. Mercy is when wrath is deserved but spared.

When the angel Gabriel told Mary that she would conceive and give birth to a son, whom she would name Jesus, she wondered how this would be, since she was a virgin. The book of Luke reveals that the angel explained that the Holy Spirit would overshadow Mary, that she would conceive a Holy Child, the Son of God. Mary received a promise that her son would receive the throne of David for eternity.

On the day Mary conceived by the Holy Spirit, the eternal God identified as a human man. Jesus participated in creation, and through Mary the miraculous union of God and man was fulfilled. Mary's son is the Son of God and the Son of Man, truly God and truly man, both divine and human for all eternity. Mary's son, Jesus, is the treasure of heaven.

The Paralytic

Proverbs {18:24} A man [that hath] friends must shew himself friendly: and there is a friend [that] sticketh closer than a brother.

WE ALL WOULD BENEFIT FROM A FRIEND IN OUR LIFE WHO can hold us accountable for our sin. The kind of friend who will not sit in judgment of us, tell others how we are struggling, or turn their back on us. It is so rare to find a faithful friend who genuinely cares about us, throughout all our good and tough times. A friend who is willing to bring us to Jesus, and help in time of need, is hard to find.

Mark 2:1-12 reveals how the paralytic's faithful friends brought him to Jesus. They found success by climbing on the housetop where Jesus was, so to let their friend down through the tiling to be near Jesus.

Jesus not only healed the paralytic but he forgave him of his sins. The Jews who heard this became uncomfortable with the idea that Jesus made himself equal to God.

Jesus has the power to forgive sins. Jesus demonstrated this power to the people with signs and miracles, to authenticate his identity as the Messiah during his ministry on earth.

What a wonderful friend we have in Jesus. The Holy Spirit has been poured out on all who have received faith for the forgiveness of sin. The Holy Spirit is our helper, protector, comforter, guide, gift-giver, and friend. May the Spirit give wisdom to serve well with like-minded friends.

Joshua of Beth-Shemesh

1 Samuel {6:14} And the cart came into the field of Joshua, a Beth-shemite, and stood there.

THE PHILISTINES DEFEATED ISRAEL AND CAPTURED THE ark of the covenant, placing it in their temple beside their god Dagon. The following morning Dagon was found face down before the ark. The next day Dagon fell again, this time suffering broken arms and head.

While in possession of the ark, the Philistines experienced afflictions and they became desperate to return the ark to Israel. To see if the ark was truly the cause of Philistine's calamity and not some coincidence, they devised a test. Two milk cows that had never been yoked were to be yoked and sent on their way with a cart carrying the ark of the covenant and a guilt offering of gold for God.

The expectation was that the milk cows would struggle against each other, since they had never been yoked, and they would make their way back to their calves. If the cows brought the ark back to its rightful owners, then there would be no question that the God of the Israelites was responsible.

There was no coincidence, the milk cows brought the ark home and came to the field of Joshua of Beth-Shemesh. Like the men who rejoiced at the return of the ark, Jesus rejoices at the return of sinners to God. From the moment of birth, sinners are captured by the enemy of sin and death. Jesus's holy life offers the return to God in victory by faith.

The Brother of Solomon

Ecclesiastes {3:1} To every [thing there is] a season, and a time to every purpose under the heaven.

SOMETIMES FAITHFUL PEOPLE GET TANGLED UP IN SIN AND suffer. King David privately ordered the murder of one of his top soldiers to cover up an adulterous affair with that soldier's wife. David married the widow, and her first son, the brother of Solomon, became ill and died as a punishment from God. David prayed that God would spare the life of Solomon's brother, he was contrite on the ground and would not eat.

When King David learned that his son was dead, he lifted himself from the ground, he washed, he ate, and he went out and worshiped God. David understood that God is good no matter what. God has a plan and has determined to execute that plan. It was not in God's will to save the baby; however, God did forgive David, who had a repentant, contrite heart and a lowly spirit.

David understood that there is a time and place for everything. David's son Solomon would go on to write a fitting narrative explaining how God has a purpose for everything under heaven. It was not God's will to spare the brother of Solomon and it was not God's will to spare his own Son, Jesus. In every season of life, whether we are young or aged, working or resting, sorrowful or happy, believers should recognize that they are in a season of sin and desperately need Jesus.

Jehoiachin

2 Kings {25:27} And it came to pass during the captivity of Jehoiachin king of Judah, [that] Evil-merodach king of Babylon in the year that he began to reign did lift up the head of Jehoiachin king of Judah out of prison. (Some dates were removed for the sake of space.)

THE LAST KING TO REIGN OVER JUDAH WAS THE EVIL JEHOI-achin. Jehoiachin tasted God's wrath after reigning for just three months. Jehoiachin watched as Nebuchadnezzar, king of Babylon, carried off the kingdom treasures and made him a pitiful prisoner. After a long time, what seems like a miracle happened that changed the life of Jehoiachin. Evil-merodach set Jehoiachin free to have a blessed life for the rest of his days.

Jehoiachin was shown grace. Only Jesus can fathom the unexplainable generosity of grace. The knowledge that an allowance of grace is offered through Jesus Christ daily merits awe-inspiring wonder. The life of the sinless Son of God, who purchased of your gift of eternal life and released you from the prison of sin and death, is priceless. There was nothing special about Jehoiachin, and there is nothing special about any who receive the gift of grace.

Jehoiachin was shown mercy. Only Jesus can realize the enormity of mercy. The very thought of mercy compels believers to grieve their own sin. Terror will fill unbelievers who will be condemned as rebels in the great judgment to come because of bondage in the prison of sin. Sin must be punished by eternal death. Mercy comes at the incredible cost of Jesus's life.

Barzillai the Gileadite

Nehemiah {7:63} And of the priests: the children of Habaiah, the children of Koz, the children of Barzillai, which took [one] of the daughters of Barzillai the Gileadite to wife, and was called after their name. {7:64} These sought their register [among] those that were reckoned by genealogy, but it was not found: therefore were they, as polluted, put from the priesthood.

PEOPLE WHO ARE CONSIDERED FOR ROLES OF IMPORTANCE must be qualified and prepared to dress the part. When the Lord brought Israel back to Jerusalem, Nehemiah's census revealed that Barzillai the Gileadite was not qualified to be a priest because he could not prove his Levitical heritage. The garments of the priesthood and the roles of importance for God would be removed.

Barzillai was certain that he was a Levite; however, without proof he was not qualified. Barzillai and believers everywhere have the same problem. No one is qualified to perform a role of importance to the glory of God without proper identification and dress for the part.

Being clothed in the righteousness of Jesus allows the faithful to dress the part. The faithful put aside their own role in exchange for the role of importance that is doing God's will. Christians are qualified to share the gospel and do good works for the Lord because of grace. Garments of grace and accessories of holiness are worn in the perfect pedigree of Jesus, when the faithful take up their cross and follow him.

Shemaiah of Nehelam

Jeremiah {29:31} Send to all them of the captivity, saying, Thus saith the LORD concerning Shemaiah the Nehelamite; Because that Shemaiah hath prophesied unto you, and I sent him not, and he caused you to trust in a lie.

OFTEN IT IS HARD TO KNOW WHO TO TRUST. EVER SINCE the garden of Eden, false prophets have tried to get people to trust God's enemy. False prophets tell lies and give false comfort to a lost world.

Shemaiah of Nehelam delivered a false letter to the Jews exiled in Babylon. Shemaiah's letter was sent in response to God's message delivered by the prophet Jeremiah. Shemaiah falsely declared God's next appointed priest and demanded that Jeremiah be punished for his directions.

Jeremiah directed Israel to settle in under Babylon rule for seventy years. God promised that when Israel once again called out to pray, God would show his name and holiness to his people. God promised to restore Israel in fulfillment of a perfect plan for them, to give them a future and hope. The Israelites were to pray for Babylon's prosperity, to grow their families, to live off the land, and to not trust false prophets.

God punished Shemaiah and will punish all who reject the gospel. Jesus warns of wolves in sheep's clothing, false prophets that distract people from the gospel. Pray for wisdom in the Spirit to share the gospel with lost people, so they are not left with a false hope from the enemy.

Hannah

1 Samuel {1:9} So Hannah rose up after they had eaten in Shiloh, and after they had drunk. Now Eli the priest sat upon a seat by a post of the temple of the LORD. {1:10} And she [was] in bitterness of soul, and prayed unto the LORD, and wept sore.

WHEN UNDER EXTREME TENSION, AT THE BREAKING POINT, what do you tend to do? Do you yell and scream or give up? It is a real choice to radiate grace and go to God in prayer when tried.

Hannah faced an emotional trial that exposed weakness. With the choice to respond with anger or grace, Hannah chose to be humble and cast her cares upon her loving God, whom she knew cared. Hannah was provoked by her husband Elkanah's second wife, Peninnah, because Hannah could not bear him children. During their annual pilgrimage to Shiloh, where they would go to worship and sacrifice to the Lord, Hannah was tormented.

In the temple, Eli saw Hannah's distress and prayed that God would grant her petition. God did grant Hannah's petition, and she bore a son named Samuel. When Samuel was old enough to be lent to the Lord, Hannah honored her vow to dedicate her son to the work of the Lord at Shiloh. Every year during pilgrimage, Hannah brought Samuel new handmade garments.

God used Hannah in his redemptive plan in Israel's history. Samuel became a great prophet and anointed King David, whom the Lord Jesus was a promised descendant.

The Shrewd Lepers

*2 Kings{7:9} Then they said one to another, We do not
well: this day [is] a day of good tidings, and we hold
our peace: if we tarry till the morning light, some mis-
chief will come upon us: now therefore come, that we
may go and tell the king's household.*

TAKING ADVANTAGE OF HIDDEN OPPORTUNITIES IN LIFE
requires the ability to be perceptive, to use sound judgment,
and to act diplomatically. Clever individuals recognize a good
thing when they see it, take full advantage for themselves, and
they do well when they share their good fortune.

During a time of unspeakable famine in Israel, the
prophet Elisha prophesied that within a twenty-four-hour
period Israel's economy would be restored. God used four
lepers, who sought a chance at life by seeking food from the
enemy, to make a promising find that fulfilled prophecy. The
lepers found that the enemy camp was abandoned and full
of riches, so they took advantage of the situation. They used
good judgment, took for themselves, and shared with the king.

Jesus taught a parable that parallels this account of the
shrewd lepers. An unjust steward learned that he was to be
unemployed, so during his last days in office he settled his master's debts in a manner that ensured that his master's debtors
would provide for him. The master commended the shrewd-
ness of the unjust steward, not for cheating but for insight.
When we share the gospel, and our assets, with those who
God loves, we have hope to be well received for our generosity.

Diotrephes

3 John {1:9} I wrote unto the church: but Diotrephes,
who loveth to have the preeminence among them,
receiveth us not.

POWER-HUNGRY, STATUS-SEEKING INDIVIDUALS WHO pursue their will, instead of God's will, in a church setting must be disciplined. The discipline of a leader who has abused his or her power of authority in church matters must be done quickly, lovingly, and firmly.

Unfortunately, many church members around the world have encountered a church bully. It takes a very strong-willed believer to make things right for the glory of the Lord. Diotrephes was a leader in the early church who abused power to the detriment of the believers in his local church.

Diotrephes's patterns of being power-hungry and status-seeking are like the patterns of the enemy of God himself, Satan. Enemies of the church push to get others to follow a poor pattern, throw out those in opposition, spread lies about believers, reject fellow Christians, hold back on provisions, and desire to have first-place status. Diotrephes exemplified the enemy of the church.

Do not be surprised if you encounter someone who says that they follow Christ; however, they do not keep in step with the Spirit. Come before the Lord in prayer, knowing that this is not the first time God has heard this plea. By the lead of the Spirit, in accordance with scripture, the body of Christ must discipline church bullies, share the gospel, and grow the kingdom of heaven.

Cana

Matthew {22:8} Then saith he to his servants,
The wedding is ready, but they which were
bidden were not worthy.

ONE OF THE MOST WONDERFUL THINGS ABOUT A WEDDING celebration is the revelation of the bride. The wedding day is the one day that the bride will make every attempt to look her loveliest, to wear her best dress, and be ready to receive esteem when she is revealed.

The groom is the one to be congratulated because he has won his lovely bride. The bride could have chosen another; however, she chose her groom. The groom is the victor as he weds his intended. The ceremony of pure promises and love celebrate a mirror relation between the church and God.

Jesus chose Cana in Galilee to reveal his first miracle. In Jesus's approval of the covenant of marriage he attended a wedding. Jesus's mother became concerned because the wine ran out. Mary offered Jesus the opportunity to help. Jesus generously and miraculously turned six twenty- or thirty-gallon jugs of water into the best wine so to bless the celebration.

Unspeakable joy will fill the hearts of the church family at Jesus's wedding, and all are invited. God requires that Jesus's bride, the church, is clothed with the righteousness of Jesus Christ by the power of the Holy Spirit. The bride of Christ depends on Jesus alone, not on good works. Those who try to come based on their own good works, without faith in Jesus, are not welcome.

Chapter 5

———◆◈◆———

Song of Songs
{2:11} For, lo, the winter
is past, the rain is over [and]
gone; {2:12} The flowers appear on the earth;
the time of the singing[of birds] is come,
and the voice of the turtle is
heard in our land.

Joanna

Proverbs {11:4} Riches profit not in the day of wrath: but righteousness delivereth from death.

TYPICALLY, COMFORTABLE PEOPLE ARE UNWILLING TO exchange their identity for a new identity that is in any way less comfortable. Followers of Jesus exchange their own ambition and possessions for the service of the Lord.

Joanna is recorded in the gospel of Luke as the wife of the household manager for Herod, whose father, Herod the Great, was called King of the Jews. Herod the Great saw Jesus as a rival threat, so he hated Jesus. Joanna and her husband likely lived a lifestyle of power, status, and influence.

When Joanna met Jesus, she was healed, so she exchanged her comfortable, wealthy lifestyle and social status for a less comfortable way of following Jesus. Joanna followed Jesus to the cross and to the empty tomb. The life of Joanna reveals that the gospel has the power to destroy social bias and class barriers for people who love Jesus.

For many, the plan of exchanging their life for a life of service to Jesus is too hard. Consider the account of the rich young ruler found in the gospel of Mark. The rich young ruler felt he had followed the laws perfectly, so there was nothing left to grant him eternal life. Jesus told him to sell all he had and give to the poor, then follow him.

The rich young ruler turned away from Jesus to keep worldly wealth. Joanna turned away from worldly wealth in exchange for Jesus and eternal life.

Toi

2 Samuel {8:9} When Toi king of Hamath heard that
David had smitten all the host of Hadadezer, {8:10}
Then Toi sent Joram his son unto king David, to salute
him, and to bless him.

IN EVERY AREA OF THE WORLD ONE THING STANDS OUT AS
commonplace—there are battles everywhere. Strategic alli-
ances are often formed to maintain a sense of identity while
simultaneously achieving specific objectives.

King David had been formally anointed as king over Israel
when he took courage and approached God in a humble
prayer. *2 Samuel {7:18} "Who am I, O Lord GOD, and what is
my house, that you have brought me thus far?"* God promised
that The Holy Spirit would never leave David, and that David's
kingdom would be eternal.

As the king of Israel, David sought to conquer the territory
God promised his ancestors, and the Lord showed him great
success. King Toi recognized an opportunity to infer a strategic
alliance with King David, so he sent his son with well wishes for
peace, blessing, and health, and offered valuable gifts. King David
accepted this honor and dedicated the generous gifts to the Lord.

King Toi humbly sent his son to form a strategic alliance
with David. David humbled himself to God, recognizing his
unworthiness of God's favor. Believers also feel unworthy
that God's only Son, Jesus, came to battle our enemy of sin
and death at the cross. Jesus's strategic alliance with believers
brings peace by exchanging sin for righteousness. Believers
keep their individuality, while simultaneously being conformed into the image of Jesus, by the Spirit, in sanctification.

The Father of the Boy

Mark {9:24} And straightway the father of the child cried out, and said with tears, Lord, I believe; help thou mine unbelief.

THE FATHER OF THE BOY KNEW THAT JESUS WAS A GIFTED healer, and he brought his son to Jesus to be healed. The boy had what was thought to be an unclean spirit because he was deaf, mute, and had seizures. The father asked Jesus's disciples to heal his boy, but they were unable.

In an effort of desperation, the father sought Jesus, wondering if Jesus could help. Jesus replied that "All things are possible for those who believe." The father of the boy did what believers should do when desperately in need—come to Jesus, let the request be made known, and let God act. Jesus commanded the unclean spirit to come out of the boy and to never return. Jesus confided in his disciples that the father's boy was healed by the power of prayer.

Prayer should be made in faith, for God's will and wisdom, with an upright heart, in thanksgiving, and persistence. In Luke 18, Jesus tells a parable about a persistent widow who petitioned a judge who neither feared God nor man. This judge continually refused the widow; however, she kept coming back until she wore him out. At last, the judge granted her petition for justice against her adversary. Jesus made the point that if the unjust judge gave in to the persistent widow, honoring her request, then God's own people would surely receive his justice.

The Widow with a Jar of Oil

2 Kings {4:7} Then she came and told the man of God.
And he said, Go, sell the oil, and pay thy debt, and live
thou and thy children of the rest.

IN ANCIENT DAYS, TO BE A WIDOW WAS A REPROACH, AND to be a childless widow was disgraceful.

The widow with a jar of oil was in an exceedingly difficult circumstance and came to the prophet Elisha for help. She was in debt and could not pay the price, so her sons were to be taken away to pay the debt. By faith, the widow did what Elisha told her to do. The widow gathered as many vessels as she could, took them into her home, closed the windows and doors, and followed direction. With one pot of oil, she filled every vessel that she could find. The widow poured out oil until she ran out of vessels to fill. There was enough to sell and pay the debt and live.

The widow did not suffer as she paid the debt as a price for the lives of her sons, this was God's gift. Likewise, spiritually bankrupt, repentant sinners, who come to God for help do not pay a price to take away the reproach of sin. The Father sent the Son, in the power of the Holy Spirit, to take away the disgrace of sinful humanity. Jesus paid the price for our redemption from death. Jesus satisfied our sin debt by his anointing work on the cross, so we may live.

The Man at the Pool

John {5:8} Jesus saith unto him, Rise, take up thy bed, and walk. {5:9} And immediately the man was made whole, and took up his bed, and walked: and on the same day was the sabbath.

AMONG MANY OTHER THINGS, THE MOSAIC LAW REVEALED to the Israelites the holiness of God and the seriousness of sin. God's people were to live in a way that was different from the rest of the nations of the world. God gave Moses the ten commandments, many laws for righteousness, as well as a cycle to regulate how they would worship.

The fourth commandment—"Remember the Sabbath and keep it holy"—was intended to offer peace and rest for God's people on the seventh day of each week; however, the Jewish leaders redefined the nature of work. Jewish leaders sought to kill Jesus for healing on the Sabbath.

On one Sabbath, the Jewish leaders noticed a man who was a cripple for thirty-eight years. This man would lay near a pool hoping to be healed. Jesus healed the man completely on the Sabbath and told him to carry his bed away. Jewish leaders asked the man at the pool why he worked on the Sabbath by carrying his bed. The man at the pool usurped their power by redirecting their question to Jesus because he had the authority to heal. The man at the pool is a reminder of how Jesus is our ultimate power and authority, over and above all man-made traditions.

Goliath

*1 Samuel {17:50} So David prevailed over the
Philistine with a sling and with a stone, and smote
the Philistine, and slew him; but [there was] no
sword in the hand of David.*

ISRAEL WAS AT WAR WITH PHILISTIA. GOLIATH OF GATH
was a giant, warmongering Philistine. For forty days, Goliath brazenly taunted the God of the universe by defying the armies of the nation of Israel. Goliath wanted one Israelite soldier to come fight him to the death, and the winner's nation would receive the loser's nation as servants.

Not a single soldier in God's army was willing to fight Goliath. King Saul offered great riches, tax-exempt status, and his daughter in marriage to the Israelite who would take away the reproach and kill the giant. Amid the trembling there was a young Israelite shepherd named David who was willing to fight Goliath. David was delivering supplies to his brothers when he learned of Goliath's affront. As a shepherd, David fought off lions and bears from sheep in God's strength, and he was confident God would fight for him. David defeated Goliath.

Goliath reminds of the terrors of sin and eternal death. The faithful are victorious over sin and death because Jesus fought the battle and won. Jesus's victory at the cross offers grace, mercy, forgiveness of sins, and eternal life for all who will believe. Do you trust that Jesus fought your sin battle against death at the cross and was victorious?

Josiah

2 Kings {22:19} Because thine heart was tender, and thou hast humbled thyself before the LORD, when thou heardest what I spake against this place, and against the inhabitants thereof, that they should become a desolation and a curse, and hast rent thy clothes, and wept before me; I also have heard [thee,] saith the LORD.

So often the Bible collects dust on a bookshelf or is displayed as a divine decoration or is held as an afterthought to a religious rally, when all the while the words inside are alive and powerful.

In the days of King Josiah, who became king at the age of eight years old, Israel neglected God and fell into idolatrous sin. Josiah was a good king, with a tender heart toward God, even seeking to repair the temple. During the temple restoration, the high priest found the book of the law and it was read aloud to King Josiah. King Josiah was devastated at Israel's failure to honor God and demanded more information from God. The priest and his men went to the prophetess Hulda for a message from God.

Since King Josiah humbled himself, Hulda revealed God's promise that judgment would be delayed. King Josiah removed idol worship from God's temple, encouraged God's law to be read aloud, and restored the Passover. During Jesus's earthly ministry he too removed idol worship from God's temple, read God's law aloud, and Jesus humbled himself to go to the cross to take the punishment that restores humanity to God as the Passover lamb.

The Threshing Floor

Psalm {1:1} Blessed [is] the man that walketh not in the counsel of the ungodly, nor standeth in the way of sinners, nor sitteth in the seat of the scornful. {1:4} The ungodly [are] not so: but [are] like the chaff which the wind driveth away.

IN THIS WORLD OF LIFESTYLE CHOICES, GOD ONLY CARES to bless one. The only lifestyle choice that God cares about is how a person esteems Jesus because this choice makes an eternal difference. Is the person for or against Jesus? The threshing floor will be a place of revelation.

The harvest was gathered at the threshing floor to separate the wheat from the chaff. The chaff was attached to the wheat so both had to be beaten down and moved with a fork so that the wind could blow away the chaff, leaving the wheat for consumption. The threshing floor was a place for the judgment between the good and bad.

When left to us, our lifestyle choices will be selfish. God offers a lifestyle choice of following Jesus and trusting in his perfect work at the cross.

Jesus perfectly followed the law because we cannot. God the Father knows who esteem Jesus and follow him by living a life that is pleasing to the Father.

Those whose lifestyle choices deny Jesus will be blown away like the chaff on the threshing floor, separated from God forever. Those who deny themselves for Jesus will be blessed and gathered to God at the threshing floor, treasured forever by Jesus.

Barnabas

1 Thessalonians {5:11} Wherefore comfort yourselves together, and edify one another, even as also ye do.

ENCOURAGING THE LORD'S PEOPLE IS ONE OF THE MOST rewarding things a person can do. Believers benefit from encouragement, regardless of the greatness or smallness of their contribution.

Barnabas is described in Acts 11 as a good man, a man of encouragement, full of the Holy Spirit with great faith. Barnabas sold a piece of land and brought the proceeds to the apostles to be used for church needs. Barnabas was named by the apostles, translated "son of encouragement."

Barnabas was responsible for helping the Apostle Paul, formerly Saul of Tarsus, into the fold of the disciples. It was hard for the disciples to believe that a Jewish Roman citizen, who sought the murder of Christians, was now an apostle of the Lord Jesus Christ. Barnabas believed Paul and encouraged the other disciples to trust him.

Barnabas was a missionary to the harvest of people who would be called the first Christians and is credited for bringing a great number of people to faith in the Lord Jesus Christ.

Having someone like Barnabas in our lives to encourage us in our faith is priceless. The more we grow in our faith of Jesus the more we can be used to be an encouragement. Sacrificially give to the work of the Lord with a generous spirit, like Barnabas, with great faith and joy. The more we encourage others, the more we will find our encouragement in the Holy Spirit.

Abel

Genesis {4:9} And the LORD said unto Cain, Where [is] Abel thy brother? And he said, I know not: [Am] I my brother's keeper? {4:10} And he said, What hast thou done? the voice of thy brother's blood crieth unto me from the ground.

INDIVIDUALS WHO ARE IN THE HABIT OF DEVOTING THEMselves to the Lord by being conformed to the likeness of Jesus, by the power of the Holy Spirit, have a sincere desire to give acceptable offerings to God. Abel was a man who loved God and knew how to bring an acceptable offering.

Abel was a son of Adam and Eve, the very first people created by God. Genesis gives the account of a day when God requested both Abel and his brother Cain to bring an offering. God favored Abel's offering and rejected Cain's, angering Cain enough to murder his brother Abel.

The voice of Abel's blood cried out to God because his life was unjustly stolen to the grave by one whose deeds were evil. Unlike the cry of Abel's blood, which cried for vengeance and condemnation, the precious blood of Jesus cries for pardon.

Christians know that they are guilty of being sinful rebels to God who are declared righteous and pardoned from death by faith. Christians who love God's goodness are rejected, and many around the world become martyrs for the Lord. Abel loved God's goodness and he was the first martyr recorded. Since then, millions have gone to the grave as martyrs for living lives that are pleasing to God.

The Baptism

Romans {6:3} Know ye not, that so many of us as were baptized into Jesus Christ were baptized into his death? {6:4} Therefore we are buried with him by baptism into death: that like as Christ was raised up from the dead by the glory of the Father, even so we also should walk in newness of life.

IT IS NOTHING LESS THAN ASTONISHING TO FULLY COM-prehend God's desire to glorify people. The God who created the world, and everything in it, has no need for any of it, yet creation brings God glory and joy.

Jesus offers a new heart in the baptism of the Holy Spirit, and a journey of a life of daily spiritual cleansing from sin until entering eternal glory in heaven. The Father plunges believers into Jesus's death to sin, cleanses them, and raises them from the water to new life, lived to God's glory by the power of the Spirit. This new life deserves a public demonstration. The outward physical representation of the inward spiritual conversion is evidenced by the symbolic application of water in the presence of the church.

Consider the loving couple who wish to marry. They made a commitment to forsake all others, to love and cherish, in sickness and in health. Now imagine this loving couple deciding to keep their vows a secret. Surely there will be a public demonstration of love and commitment for the bride and groom. The declaration is the same for Jesus and the church. May water baptism, in accordance with scripture, be honored as a public ordinance of the church.

Elizabeth

Luke {1:60} And his mother answered and said,
Not [so;] but he shall be called John.

ELIZABETH AND HER HUSBAND, ZECHARIAH, WERE KNOWN
to be righteous before the Lord and blameless in their walk.
Joy came with sadness in the Lord for Elizabeth, as she lived
under reproach in her community. Elizabeth was barren and
advanced in years.

Elizabeth's faithfulness resulted in even greater gladness and joy when she discovered that she was expecting a
baby. The angel Gabriel gave the news to Elizabeth's husband,
Zechariah, in God's holy temple. Zechariah was struck mute
for lack of faith. Elizabeth's baby would be named John, he
would be filled with the Holy Spirit. John would turn hearts
to God and prepare the way for the Messiah.

There was to be rejoicing for Elizabeth and her cousin.
Mary, who was a virgin, was also visited by the angel. Mary's
baby would inherit the throne of King David to reign forever,
as Lord and Savior; and her cousin Elizabeth's baby son was
to announce his arrival.

Elizabeth's son, John, is among the first recorded to leap
for joy at the coming of the Savior, and he did so from his
mother's womb. When the time came to name the baby at
the temple and for circumcision, Elizabeth was the one to
declare his name because her husband was unable to speak.
Once Elizabeth declared John's name, Zechariah miraculously
spoke and praised God.

Nathanael

John {1:46} And Nathanael said unto him, Can there
any good thing come out of Nazareth?

PEOPLE TEND TO SURROUND THEMSELVES WITH INDIVIDU-
als who have acceptable reputations based on their own
confirmation bias.

Nathanael was a disciple of Jesus who was looking for the
coming Messiah. Jesus was known to have lived in Nazareth,
a detestable town. Nathanael's experience with the reputation
of Nazareth led him to be skeptical that the Messiah would
have lived in such a repulsive place.

When Jesus spoke to Nathanael for the first time, he realized that Jesus was different. Jesus revealed that he knew that
Nathanael was prejudiced against the people of Nazareth.
Nathanael put his bias aside and followed Jesus, believing
him to be the Son of God.

During the time of Jesus, the reputation of Nazareth was
not quite as bad as the reputation of Samaria. Samaritans
were regarded as inferior Jewish descendants. In response to
Jesus's command to love your neighbor as yourself, an expert
in the law asked Jesus to define his neighbor. The lawyer likely
hoped to exclude certain people from his lifestyle.

Luke 10, Jesus's parable answer: A man was traveling when
he was robbed, beaten, and left for dead. Both a Jewish priest
and a Levite, traveling separately, crossed the road to avoid
the man. The good Samaritan stopped, provided medical aid,
brought the man to an inn, and paid the entire bill for his
recovery. Our neighbor is anyone who can receive God's love,
and we are to love without prejudice.

The Water

*Matthew {14:25} And in the fourth watch of the night
Jesus went unto them, walking on the sea.*

AMONG FACTS, SCRIPTURE IS FULL OF IMAGERY, META-
phors, similes, personifications, and hyperboles. God has
creatively conveyed the word "water," used repeatedly, in all
these literary features. Water reveals God's desire to intervene
with creation to provide blessing and judgment.

Water is necessary for life with refreshment, cleansing,
and growth. Water is powerful and can change topography,
used for punishment in Noah's day, and is poured out in sacrifice. The Spirit of God hovered over the face of the waters
at creation. Creation must have water to exist.

Sin always finds a wave into the human heart. Satan aims
to distract believers so that they will replace the good water
with bad. An ungrateful attitude toward God, who is the
fountain of living water, will bring brokenness to believers
who are not careful to thirst after Jesus, the pure supply.

Like rain that drops and distills as dew or like tender
showers on the earth, God's Word is absorbed in the hearts
of the faithful. The same water that trembled and parted for
the Israelites as they fled from Egypt, supported the Savior
as he walked on top of it.

Whether you are flooded with the wretched waters of tears
or refreshed with cold water to a weary soul, remember, living
water is always near. The more that God's faithful quench their
thirst with Jesus, the less they will overlook God's desire to
flood their hearts with joy.

Chapter 6

Psalm {89:36}
His seed shall
endure for ever,
and his throne
as the sun before me.

Lydia

*Acts {16:14} And a certain woman named Lydia, a seller
of purple, of the city of Thyatira, which worshipped
God, heard [us:] whose heart the Lord opened, that she
attended unto the things which were spoken of Paul.*

WHEN A PERSON PURSUES SUCCESS FOR A LIFE OF PLENTY,
they know that there are no shortcuts, easy paths, or hand-
outs. Successful people are happy to work hard to realize their
goals and dreams.

The Apostle Paul and his colleague Silas obeyed God,
who in a vision compelled a mission to share the gospel in
Macedonia. As a result of their obedience, God opened the
heart of Lydia, who is the first recorded person in Europe
to receive the gospel and be baptized. Lydia was hospitable,
happy to work hard, and generous with her wealth.

God's faithful may be encouraged to work hard to understand the Bible and to generously give the gospel of Jesus to
the spiritually lost. A life of plenty, for the believer, should be
full of souls that have been won over for Christ.

"Lord, with whom can I share the gospel today?" is a question to ask with expectation that God has a plan. God has
placed you here for a reason, to facilitate the growth of his
kingdom for his glory. Work hard in studying the Bible, so
that you may be generous in giving the gospel too. How many
people will you know in heaven whose hearts were opened
by God unto salvation because of you?

Araunah

Nahum {1:7} The LORD [is] good, a strong hold in the day of trouble; and he knoweth them that trust in him.

GOD WANTS HIS PEOPLE TO TRUST IN HIM EXCLUSIVELY. The opposite of trusting God would be trusting in ourselves or anything else to bring us victory in any aspect of life.

2 Samuel reveals how King David took inventory of all his fighting men. The census revealed eight hundred thousand fighting men in Israel and five hundred thousand fighting men in Judah. David realized that trusting in his census instead of trusting God was sin. God punished David for idolatry by sending an angel to destroy seventy thousand men. God stopped the angel from further destruction at the threshing floor of Araunah.

Araunah the Jebusite owned land that the king needed. God wanted David to build an altar for the Lord, to be used for burnt offerings and peace offerings. Araunah offered the land at no charge, along with wood and oxen; however, David insisted on paying for it himself. God accepted the offerings and averted the plagues. The land that Araunah sold to David was the very location that King Solomon built God's holy temple.

God's punishment for David's idolatry ended at Araunah's threshing floor. God's punishment for humanity's idolatry ended at the cross of Jesus. God is jealous for our trust. The first-created humans neglected to trust God; however, we can learn from them to only trust Jesus for the victory of forgiveness of sins and eternal life.

Mount of Beatitudes

Matthew {5:3} Blessed [are] the poor in spirit:
for theirs is the kingdom of heaven.

SIN HAS TURNED THE WORLD UPSIDE-DOWN. SO MANY things declared wrong have been declared right in both the material world and in the spiritual world. Although the faithful live in an age of gross rebellion against God, they still find blessings. The word blessing often paints an image of a perfectly satisfying godsend that fills the soul with unspeakable pleasure; however, God defines blessing a little different than man in the Beatitudes.

Jesus chose a special mountain to open his mouth and teach about how God blesses people. Believers are richly blessed in Christ when they recognize how spiritually poor they are. Grieving sin while giving thanks to Jesus for covering sin yields blessing. Meekness is often mistaken for weakness; however, blessing comes when strong-willed believers with power and position use their strength to yield to the Holy Spirit and trust God's plan.

Believers who pour out their hearts in search for God's right standard are blessed by his faithfulness. The blessing of merciful reciprocity is found when the believer relents from rightful punishment on others. Taking every thought into command to keep the heart pure is a difficult act. When done in the power of the Spirit this leads to blessing.

Jesus's purpose was to bring blessings of peace and of reconciliation. Blessings come from the expectation of personal pain for serving Jesus. Persecution awaits the faithful who look forward to future blessing. Jesus is our blessing.

James

Psalm {118:23} This is the LORD'S doing;
it [is] marvelous in our eyes.

SOME PEOPLE DO NOT BELIEVE IN HEROES AND OTHERS hide their heroism well. Genuine people who are capable of impressive feats typically do not seek accolades. By contrast, many are skeptical that someone can perform acts of heroism deserving of praise.

James grew up in the same home, ate at the same table, and learned from the same parents as Jesus. James did not believe anything was unique about his brother Jesus, as they lived together for nearly thirty years. James would not believe that his brother was the Messiah before or immediately after Jesus's earthly ministry.

It took the power of the resurrection for James to believe that Jesus was different. Jesus made a point to appear to James in new life, and James made it a point to follow Jesus.

James wrote an epistle found in the New Testament focusing on how believers with genuine faith respond to the gospel. When genuine faith is in the heart of the believer, then that faith produces good works that give God glory and blessings to others. James taught believers to reject favoritism, to tame the tongue, to seek wisdom, to not covet money, to be steadfast, to be honest, to forgive, to live in peace, to resist pride, to be patient, to pray, to restore those who stray, and to do the will of the Lord. All of this may be accomplished by the power of the Holy Spirit within.

The Queen of Sheba

Proverbs {9:10} The fear of the LORD [is] the beginning of wisdom: and the knowledge of the holy [is] understanding.

WISDOM IS THE ABILITY TO DISCERN TRUTH AND APPLY IT rightly to life. Understanding is the ability to shun evil. The world is full of people who deny wisdom and refuse understanding. Many people redefine truth to match their lifestyle, so their understanding does not offend their conscience.

The Queen of Sheba was a very wealthy ruler who was seeking God's wisdom outside of the religions of her own land. The Queen of Sheba journeyed to Jerusalem with a large entourage of camels, gold, spices, and exquisite jewels, searching for wisdom, understanding, and truth.

Solomon, the son of David, was the king of Israel, and was blessed by the Lord God with wisdom. Solomon's name was famous in all the lands for his wisdom. The Queen of Sheba had many questions and Solomon explained every truth she wanted to learn and sent her home with an even larger entourage of gifts.

The Queen of Sheba had reverence for the God of Israel and sought after his wisdom. Everyone who will believe that God exists and diligently seek truth in the Bible can know wisdom and understanding.

Every learning opportunity around us is worthless unless it is built on the foundation of the knowledge of the Lord Jesus Christ. Read the Bible to discover truth for it is God's desire to reveal himself to you. The Holy Spirit generously reveals wisdom and understanding.

Aaron

Exodus {28:1} And take thou unto thee Aaron thy brother, and his sons with him, from among the children of Israel, that he may minister unto me in the priest's office.

CHRISTIANS STRUGGLE WITH SIN. MAY WE NEVER BELIEVE that we have a handle on the epidemic of sin. Some of the dearest people in the Bible sinned against God, yet God still used them for glory.

Moses's brother Aaron served as his right-hand man. God used Aaron to speak to Pharaoh, the words God gave to Moses, during the exodus of the Jews from their slavery in Egypt. Aaron was a Levite and God chose him to be the first high priest for Israel.

God evidenced Aaron's priesthood in a miraculous way. God had each of the twelve heads of family, from the sons of Jacob, place their staff in the tabernacle in front of the ark of the covenant. The family God chose to be his royal priesthood would see a sprout on their staff the next morning. Aaron's staff, from his lineage of Levi, not only sprouted overnight, but produced flowers and almonds. God ordained that Aaron would be the first priest.

One may think Aaron was an exceptionally good person; however, before and during the role as priest, Aaron failed God. Aaron fashioned a golden calf for the Israelites to worship in the desert, and when questioned about the idol by Moses, Aaron told a half-truth. Aaron was an imperfect priest in many ways; however, Jesus is the perfect, holy priest forever.

Joseph of Arimathea

John {19:38} And after this Joseph of Arimathaea,
being a disciple of Jesus, but secretly for fear of the Jews,
besought Pilate that he might take away the body of
Jesus: and Pilate gave [him] leave. He came therefore,
and took the body of Jesus.

FEAR IS A MYSTERIOUS EMOTION, SOME HIDE FROM IT, some face it, and some are driven by it.

Joseph was a well-respected member of the Jewish council, a good, righteous, and rich man. He knew the danger of following Jesus as a public disciple, yet he did not favor the way that Jesus was delivered to Pilate to be crucified, and he feared the Jews who acted like an angry mob.

Joseph recognized that Jesus was the Messiah, and if he were to give him a burial fit for a king, then he had to make a life-changing decision fast.

Joseph faced his fears and took great courage to use his political privilege to ask Pilate for the body of Jesus. Jesus was a crucified criminal under Roman authority and a proper burial was never expected by Rome or by the Jews. Joseph of Arimathea fulfilled prophecy written in scripture regarding the Messiah, that he would die with the wicked but would be buried with the rich. God used Joseph of Arimathea to help bury the Son with honor.

The life-changing decision of the cross brings fear. Some turn to the cross and face fear of rejection from others and some hide from the cross disregarding their fear of God's judgment.

Jonathan

1 Samuel {20:18} Then Jonathan said to David, To morrow [is] the new moon: and thou shalt be missed, because thy seat will be empty.

WHEN CHOOSING A FRIEND, IT IS IMPORTANT TO LOOK AT character traits to determine if the person is worthy. Prior to choosing a friend, it is important to examine the person's reputation for honesty, trustworthiness, and loyalty. Jonathan was King Saul's son, and he chose his friend David wisely.

David loved Jonathan and Jonathan loved David. Jonathan gave David his own robe and military gear. As David prospered, Jonathan's father, King Saul, grew jealous. Jonathan's dear friend and brother-in-law David was a threat to his father's rule because he was the anointed one to be the next king of Israel.

Jonathan conspired to warn David of his father's desire to kill him after seeing David's seat empty at the king's table. David's life was spared thanks to his loyal friend Jonathan. David repaid Jonathan by remembering his son Mephibosheth, who was a cripple. King David honored Mephibosheth and gave him a lifelong seat, every day to eat at the king's table.

Like Jonathan made friends with David, the Holy Spirit makes friends with us; however, Jesus warns that we are only worthy of friendship with God the Father because of the cross. Jesus is worthy of friendship because his honesty is absolute, his trustworthiness is true, and his loyalty is everlasting. *Song of Songs {2:4} He brought me to the banqueting house, and his banner over me [was] love.* Is Jesus your friend?

Joseph

Genesis {45:7} And God sent me before you to preserve you a posterity in the earth, and to save your lives by a great deliverance.

JOSEPH WAS JACOB'S FAVORITE SON WHO WORE A BEAUTIful gift from his father, a colorful coat. The brothers hated Joseph for bringing their father bad reports, for being the favorite son, and for sharing dreams with the brothers; dreams that he would one day rule them.

Joseph's brothers planned to murder him; instead, they sold him as an Egyptian slave. The brothers lied to heartbroken Jacob, saying he was killed by animals, they staged a bloody coat.

God prospered Joseph and he managed Potiphar's home, until his wife falsely accused him of making advances. In prison, Joseph interpreted dreams and was remembered when the Pharaoh was tormented with dreams that no one could interpret. Joseph interpreted for Pharaoh that a generous harvest would occur over the next seven years, followed by a seven-year famine.

Joseph's family was starving, so Jacob sent ten sons to Egypt but kept his youngest son home. Joseph was manager of the harvest; they did not recognize him. Joseph accused the brothers of being spies and demanded they leave one brother in Egypt and return home to fetch their youngest brother. When the eleven brothers were together Joseph revealed himself to them.

God used Joseph to sustain the family lineage to Jesus. Jacob moved his family to be with Joseph. Israel consisted of seventy people in their move to Egypt, where there was plenty to eat.

Cornelius

Acts {10:30} And Cornelius said, Four days ago I was fasting until this hour; and at the ninth hour I prayed in my house, and, behold, a man stood before me in bright clothing, {10:31} And said, Cornelius, thy prayer is heard.

GOD REVEALED THE APOSTLE PETER'S ROLE IN BRINGING the gospel to the non-Jew/Gentile nations in a vision. Three times, God told Peter to eat from a variety of animals that were against God's law to eat because they were unclean. Each time Peter refused to eat the unclean animals, and each time God told Peter not to refuse. Peter learned that what was unclean before was now clean.

Up to this point, Israel had the exclusive rights and responsibilities to formally worship God as a chosen people. Some non-Jews with religious backgrounds would worship God in reverence; however, they too needed the gospel to be saved. Cornelius was a centurion, a Roman military officer who was a well-respected worshiper of God. Cornelius was a God-fearing man.

Peter shared the gospel with Cornelius and all his family, even though they were not God's chosen people under the law. Cornelius's family understood the gospel, received the Holy Spirit, and were baptized. The gospel simply put is that God anointed Jesus to be the Savior of the world, not just for Israel. Jesus commands followers to bring the gospel to all the nations of the world. God fulfilled the promise to Abraham to use his family to bless the nations of the world.

Caiaphas

John {11:49} And one of them, [named] Caiaphas, being the high priest that same year, said unto them, Ye know nothing at all, {11:50} Nor consider that it is expedient for us, that one man should die for the people, and that the whole nation perish not.

OCCASIONALLY, A DISRUPTION COMES ALONG THAT CREates an opportunity for a dedicated leader to act. Leaders identify problems and create solutions that benefit the greater good. An excellent leader will rally like-minded individuals and persuade them to protect their best interest at any cost.

The Jewish priests were following the laws of Moses and enjoyed a rich lifestyle as a result. In the best interest of the priesthood, any conversation that would eliminate the role of temple sacrifice was to be considered as a disruption and acted on accordingly.

Jesus proved to be the Son of God by performing miraculous signs; however, he was not viewed as Israel's political victor over Roman rule. If Jesus was the Jewish Christ King, then the priest role of temple sacrifice would be unnecessary, and the Jews would be regarded as traitors to Rome.

Caiaphas rallied the Jews to riot when Jesus publicly declared himself to be the Son of God, so to solve a disruptive problem that would eliminate the priesthood. Caiaphas foretold the fate of Jesus with the solution to keep Israel at status quo; however, Jesus went to the cross with the intent to protect his best interest, to reconcile sinners to God.

Sapphira

*Acts {5:10} Then fell she down straightway at his feet,
and yielded up the ghost: and the young men came in,
and found her dead, and, carrying [her] forth, buried
[her] by her husband.*

HYPOCRISY IS TO PROCLAIM A SPECIFIC BELIEF AND THEN
behave in a contradictory manner.

Sapphira and her husband, Ananias, were a part of the
early church in Jerusalem. These early believers were so filled
by the Holy Spirit that they operated as if they all had one
mind and one heart. Out of their love for Jesus and faith in
God's provision, they willingly sold all that they had and gave
it all to the church. Church leadership would distribute the
wealth as needed, so that none were without.

Sapphira and her husband sold their land; however, they
held back some of their money but told that they gave all.
Sapphira conspired with her husband and lied to Peter and
to God. As a result, both she and her husband died. Jesus
warns us against hypocrisy in this account of protecting the
early church from sin.

Expect temptation to sin to be constant in your day-to-
day life. God is holy, he hates sin, and he always disciplines
the beloved church. The scriptures say that if God does not
discipline you, then you are not his legitimate son or daughter.

Sin is serious, may we take it seriously. May we never
test the Holy Spirit. When we sin, may we immediately
seek out our loving Father in heaven for forgiveness. Jesus
is faithful to forgive.

The Repentant Criminal

*Luke {23:42} And he said unto Jesus, Lord,
remember me when thou comest into thy kingdom.
{23:43} And Jesus said unto him, Verily I say unto thee,
To day shalt thou be with me in paradise.*

THE CORRUPT NATURE OF HUMANITY MAKES IT IMPOSSIBLE for a person to initiate a meaningful relationship with God. No matter how kind, helpful, patient, and gentle the Holy Spirit is in calling humankind, some will not respond. A human heart can only be turned to Jesus by God's grace. God instills the desire in the hearts of people to exercise free will to repent and be saved.

On the cross Jesus hung between two criminals who were unable to escape from the devil's snare, each being punished for doing the devil's will. Both criminals observed the rioting mob, the unusual brutality of Jesus, and the most undeserved punishment in history. Both criminals witnessed Jesus's kindness in praying for the accusers, the care shown to Jesus's mother, the patient agony, and Jesus's will to die. Grace was at work for one of the two criminals.

The repentant criminal recognized Jesus as God's suffering servant and found repentance as a dying man. By God's grace, the criminal came to his senses, received the gift of faith unto salvation, and escaped the eternal snare of the devil. The repentant criminal did not get baptized, and he did no good works, yet Jesus saved him from sin and death. God calls people as he will, so never give up hope for the unsaved.

Judas Iscariot

Mark {14:10} And Judas Iscariot, one of the twelve, went unto the chief priests, to betray him unto them.

JUDAS ISCARIOT WAS ONE OF THE TWELVE DISCIPLES OF Jesus and overseer of their money. Jesus knew that Judas would betray, fulfilling prophecy written long before Judas was born. Judas walked with Jesus, witnessed signs and miracles, and heard the teachings. Judas even experienced the humble service of Jesus washing his feet and the feet of every disciple before the Passover feast.

Judas Iscariot was disloyal; he was a false friend, full of greed and deceit. In his own free will, Judas betrayed the Son of God for thirty pieces of silver, which he shamefully tried to return and then hung himself on a tree in his unrepentant guilt.

Jesus knew that his hour had come to pay the ultimate price for the forgiveness of sins. Jesus's disciples were troubled that Jesus advised that they had an enemy in their inner circle. All the disciples questioned their own conviction on whether it was them who would betray Jesus.

The best way to avoid betraying God is by keeping a right relationship with Jesus. Jesus taught that many would come to him in the end thinking that they are saved by their good works; however, Jesus will send them away because they were never known by him. When we humble ourselves to pursue the work of the Spirit, we have hope to be loyal to and known by Jesus.

Chapter 7

Romans {12:12}
Rejoicing in hope;
patient in tribulation; continuing
instant in prayer.

Tamar

Genesis {38:11} Then said Judah to Tamar his daugh-
ter in law, Remain a widow at thy father's house, till
Shelah my son be grown: for he said, Lest peradventure
he die also, as his brethren [did.] And Tamar went and
dwelt in her father's house.

THE BIBLE TRACES THE LINEAGE OF OUR LORD JESUS
Christ all the way back to Adam. Ancestry is taken very seriously in scripture because of the promise of a savior. Judah
was the son that God used to continue the Messianic line after
his father, Jacob, who was Abraham's grandson.

Judah gave his firstborn son a bride named Tamar, but the
son died. Judah commanded that his second son take Tamar
as his bride, and Tamar became widowed again. Judah then
charged Tamar to remain a widow until his third son, Shelah,
could marry; however, Judah had no intention of giving her
his son Shelah for fear that he may die like his brothers.

When Tamar realized that she was deceived she took matters into her own hands and followed Judah with the intent to
conceive by him while in disguise. When Tamar was found
to be with child, Judah commanded that she be burned for
immorality; however, Tamar revealed that the baby's father
made her a pledge, and she exposed a signet, cord, and staff
belonging to Judah.

Tamar was forgiven, and God used her first-born son,
Perez, a twin, for the purpose of continuing the family lineage
to the Messiah, The Lord and Savior, Jesus Christ.

The Garden of Gethsemane

Luke {22:44} And being in an agony he prayed more earnestly: and his sweat was as it were great drops of blood falling down to the ground.

TO BE SUCCESSFUL, ONE MUST PREPARE TO TAKE PRESSURE. Before time began, Jesus chose to die under a great deal of pressure for sinners. God sent Jesus with full knowledge that at the time of death Jesus would be wounded beyond recognition.

Gethsemane is a fitting place for Jesus to be arrested in because it means "oil press" in Hebrew. In the garden of Gethsemane, in the Mount of Olives, Jesus revealed the heartbreak and pressing anguish over the suffering to come. The full weight of the sins of the world was to be pressed on Jesus and his body reacted in a rare medical manner as he sweat great drops of blood.

Jesus prepared a garden for the man made in his image, Adam, who turned from God causing sin to enter the world. In the garden of Gethsemane, Jesus was pressed while praying in preparation for the obedient suffering that is our promised hope for eternal life.

Yet, in another garden, Jesus was properly buried in a new tomb from where God would resurrect by the power of the Spirit after three days. Our Lord was fully pressed for the sins of humanity. For his first appearance, King Jesus chose to reveal his resurrected body to a woman in the garden who mistook Jesus for a gardener. Garden after garden, glory to glory, Jesus is Lord.

Ethan

Romans {8:18} For I reckon that the sufferings of this present time [are] not worthy [to be compared] with the glory which shall be revealed in us.

SUFFERING IS THE OPPOSITE OF WHAT THE WORLD WOULD expect a believer in the good Lord Jesus to endure. "Where are you, Lord?" is the question most have while suffering. Monetary loss, family loss, and failing health are all sources that cause a person to suffer. Unfortunately, some people turn away from God when experiencing a tough time, thinking that God is not there at all.

Ethan was a wise songwriter and contributor to the book of Psalms who did not turn away from God during times of suffering. When God gave King David's enemies victory, causing Israel a shameful mockery, Ethan held tight to God's promises concerning the Messiah.

Psalm {89:18} For the LORD [is] our defense; and the Holy One of Israel [is] our king.

Ethan experienced suffering while knowing how faithful God is, how worthy of praise God is, how powerful God is, how marvelous God's character is, and how true God is to his promises.

When a person adopts the false theory that becoming a Christian will make life easy and pain-free, they are in for a rude awakening. Suffering is just as much a part of life as smiling. When the glory of God becomes the focus of the believer and living for Jesus becomes the priority during the good and tough times in life, the believer will experience true joy in the Lord.

Nathan

*2 Samuel {12:7} And Nathan said to David,
Thou [art] the man.*

TEMPTATION DOES NOT HAVE TO GET THE BEST OF US, BUT when it does, it can be tragic. The journey into deception may cause a person to fail to recognize themselves.

King David remained home while his men were at war. David allowed sin into his mind, and one unwise decision led to another.

A beautiful woman was bathing, so David sent for her, and she conceived. David covered up the crime by bringing her husband home from the battle to be with his wife, but he refused. David ordered a death sentence for that man and married his widow to cover the crime, so God sent the prophet Nathan.

Nathan delivered a message of God's judgment upon David by telling him a parable about a poor man with one precious lamb who fell victim to a rich man with his own flock. The rich man stole the poor man's lamb and David was indignant, demanding that the rich man die as a punishment. Nathan advised that David was the guilty, rich man.

David's temptation to covet led to adultery and that led to murder. David understood that his sin was against the Lord. David disgraced himself, yet his life was spared.

Pray that Jesus, the final prophet, who is God's Word, will prevent you from lingering near temptation like David, Eve, and many God-fearing people do before their disgrace. Once the sin seed is planted, temptation grows. One thing leads to another. May our one thing be prayer in Jesus's name to avoid temptation to sin.

Jason

*Acts {17:5} But the Jews which believed not, moved
with envy, took unto them certain lewd fellows of the
baser sort, and gathered a company, and set all the city
on an uproar, and assaulted the house of Jason, and
sought to bring them out to the people.*

GOD CALLS PEOPLE TO SHARE THE GOSPEL WITH THE
unsaved. Missionaries teach from the Bible, pray for believers, participate in everyday fellowship, and often they are
hated and abused.

The Apostle Paul and his colleague Silas went to a synagogue in Thessalonica together to share the gospel. Paul spent
three Sabbath days there and many Jews, Greeks, and women
believed. Jason was a man who was among those in the synagogue and believed in the gospel message. Jason welcomed
Paul and Silas into his house to offer them hospitality.

Jason and his house were assaulted for welcoming the missionaries. Jews were envious because the gospel took important
customs and roles away from the Jewish leaders. If Jesus was
declared the king, then the Jews were in jeopardy of committing
treason under the reign of King Caesar. If Jesus was the ultimate
sacrifice, then their lucrative temple offerings were finished.

Regardless of the potential hardship, like Jason, God calls
Christians to be missionaries and to welcome missionaries.
God calls some missionaries to leave their families and go to
a far-off place to work and share the gospel. God calls the rest
to make disciples of Jesus where they are.

Lot's wife

Luke {17:32} Remember Lot's wife.

THERE ARE MANY DISTRACTIONS IN THIS WORLD AND identifying patterns of selfishness can be difficult.

The people of Sodom and Gomorrah were sinful, so much so that the Lord judged and destroyed them. Abraham's brother Lot lived in Sodom with his wife and daughters. Although Lot identified with that sinful culture, his faith in God was that which was considered as righteous.

For the sake of Abraham, God sent his angels to warn Lot of impending doom for Sodom and Gomorrah. Lot and his family were rescued as God poured out his judgment for their sinfulness.

Lot and his daughters did what the angels told them to do, to run for their lives and not turn back; however, Lot's wife did not follow instructions. Lot's wife's identity was with the city she loved, and she lingered and looked behind watching the sulfur and fire falling from the sky on her beloved home. Soon Lot's wife was succumbed to the ruin, standing as a pillar of salt.

Eternal judgment comes for sinners that linger in their identification of sin, just like Lot's wife lingered behind and was lost. God rescues followers of Jesus who commit to live for God and not for themselves. One day, Jesus will return and establish a righteous kingdom, so let your identity in Christ be public. Let your identity cause you to run in a pattern toward Jesus. Turn away from selfish sin, as if your very life depends on it.

Cleopas

Luke {24:18} And the one of them, whose name was Cleopas, answering said unto him, Art thou only a stranger in Jerusalem, and hast not known the things which are come to pass there in these days?

MANY THINGS IN LIFE ARE DISCOURAGING. WHEN A GREAT disappointment threatens a severe depression, finding consolation for the soul is essential. Cleopas was a follower of Jesus, believing in the miracles with great hope that Jesus was the Jewish Messiah; however, Jesus was crucified, and all hope seemed lost.

Jesus's body and blood were still a mystery regarding the forgiveness of sins and eternal life. Jesus did not fulfill the Jewish expectation of their political Messiah. The Jews falsely accused Jesus, tried him in a Roman court where he was judged not guilty, and then insisted on sentencing God's Son to death on the cross. Naturally, Cleopas and his friend were sad.

Cleopas and his friend were walking together when they were unknowingly joined by Jesus. As they walked, Jesus explained to them the scriptures from the beginning. Jesus referenced Moses, the prophets, and the prophecies concerning the necessary suffering, death, and eternal glory of the Messiah. After the revelation of Jesus's identity to Cleopas and his friend, both felt an emotional stir of joy replace their sadness. When we are sad, may we remember how essential it is to read the Bible and rejoice. What was once a sad mystery is now the glorious hope of salvation. Does your soul find consolation in Jesus?

Micaiah

1 Kings {22:14} And Micaiah said, [As] the LORD liveth, what the LORD saith unto me, that will I speak.

PEOPLE HEAR WHAT THEY WANT TO HEAR. MOST PEOPLE will filter out messaging that does not agree with their beliefs. Many people are insisting on being their own god and doing whatever they want to do. All around the world people seek to harm believers who declare God's truth.

The divided kingdom of Israel was collaborating to conquer the city of Ramoth-gilead. The king of Israel, Ahab and the king of Judah, Jehoshaphat consulted with the prophets of the king of Israel, who promised victory; however, the king of Judah wanted a true prophet.

Micaiah was the true prophet. Micaiah declared that Ahab was trusting in lies, told by false prophets, concerning God's will for victory in the battle to conquer Ramoth-gilead. Micaiah was struck and imprisoned for speaking God's truth. As a result of trusting the enemy, Ahab died.

Jesus is the true prophet that we can trust when we battle the enemy. Ephesians, chapter 6, offers armor for the faithful soldier: A helmet to protect our thoughts, a breastplate of righteousness to protect our heart and vital organs, a sword that is the actual Spirit of God, a belt consisting of God's truth, a shield to thwart Satan's attacks, and footwear of the gospel to use when we pray and share the gospel. May God's faithful put on the full armor of God and declare God's truth.

Achan

Joshua {7:19} And Joshua said unto Achan, My son, give, I pray thee, glory to the LORD God of Israel, and make confession unto him; and tell me now what thou hast done; hide [it] not from me.

AFTER ESCAPING EGYPT AND SPENDING A GENERATION OF time wandering in the desert, the Israelites were to conquer their promised land. The first city to be conquered was Jericho. The commander of the Lord's army told Joshua to have all of Israel follow the ark of the covenant and march around the city for seven days, and on the seventh day blow the trumpets, and make a loud cry. The city walls fell.

The Israelites were to store precious stones and metals in the treasury of the house of the Lord as precious to God. Everything else was to burn to the ground, except for one faithful woman named Rahab, whom God used in the lineage to Jesus, and her family.

When the Israelites were ready to battle again, they failed and became afraid. Items that were supposed to be stored in the treasury were not, but they were stolen and secretly hidden in the camp.

The Israelites were examined, and Achan was found guilty of disobedience because he purposed to act on temptation to steal from God. Achan was stoned to death and burned with all he had.

Like Achan, Jesus was tempted to sin; however, Jesus did not sin. By prayer we cling to Jesus when tempted, he is faithful and able to help us resist sin that leads to death, so we may live.

Azariah

2 Chronicles {15:1} And the Spirit of God came upon Azariah the son of Oded: {15:2} And he went out to meet Asa, and said unto him, Hear ye me, Asa, and all Judah and Benjamin; The LORD [is] with you, while ye be with him; and if ye seek him, he will be found of you; but if ye forsake him, he will forsake you.

CORRECTING A PUBLIC OFFENSE TAKES A LOT OF COURAGE. The divided kingdom of Israel was steeped in idolatry when King Asa inherited the crown as king of Judea. Asa needed courage to remove the idols from the land because they stole glory from God and God alone was to be glorified.

God sent the prophet Azariah with a message to inspire courage and King Asa was inspired by Azariah's message from God. Asa redirected the nation's focus toward God by putting away the abominable idols that offended God, and he renewed the altar of the LORD. As a result, King Asa enjoyed many years of God's blessed peace.

It takes courage to genuinely seek after Jesus in a world that is offended by him. Believers can take courage by trusting in the Living God, King of Heaven, who holds all the power. Jesus provides courage to remove the idols from the high places in our lives. When we look to idols for comfort, for entertainment, or for security, we are robbing God of his glory. May we always guard against glorifying anyone or anything because God alone deserves all the glory.

Pontius Pilate

John {19:10} Then saith Pilate unto him, Speakest thou not unto me? knowest thou not that I have power to crucify thee, and have power to release thee?

PONTIUS PILATE HAD THE POWER TO DELIVER JESUS'S death sentence because God gave it to him for a reason. Crucifixion was Rome's lowest form of punishment, reserved for the most despised, vilest criminals of the day.

As the governor of Judea, Pontius Pilate was the only one who had the authority to deliver a death sentence for Jesus. The Jews were furious with Jesus's claim to be the Son of God and needed Pilate to remove him by death, so they formed a mob and delivered Jesus to be crucified. The priests and the elders were determined to see Jesus die to put an end to what they considered a blasphemous attempt to overthrow their Jewish law-abiding lifestyle.

The Jewish leaders did not recognize that their Messiah's kingdom was a spiritual kingdom and not an earthly kingdom. The Jews needed Pilate's Roman authority to set the crucifixion in motion, all according to God's plan.

The wage of sin is eternal death; however, not all sinners will be declared guilty for sin. God is merciful, that is why he sent the Son by the power of the Holy Spirit to be a perfect man. Jesus is qualified to take the punishment for sin in place of sinful people. Sinners may be declared not guilty because of Jesus's work at the cross.

Jacob's Ladder

*Genesis {28:12} And he dreamed, and behold a ladder
set up on the earth, and the top of it reached to heaven:
and behold the angels of God ascending and descend-
ing on it.*

SOMETIMES INDIVIDUALS VALUE THINGS SO MUCH THAT
they are willing to do anything to obtain them. Some will
even go as far as to participate in manipulation and deception. Jacob treasured the birthright to his father Isaac's lineage
because of his faith in God's promises. There was a great
blessing to be obtained from Isaac. Jacob was willing to do
anything to obtain the birthright.

Jacob was Esau's younger twin. Esau was very hungry
one day as Jacob was cooking lentils. Jacob offered the beans
in exchange for the birthright and Esau agreed. Jacob's
mother also wanted her second son to obtain the blessing. On Isaac's deathbed she had Jacob trick his father into
blessing him, instead of Esau. Jacob had to flee in fear that
Esau would kill him.

Jacob's parents sent him to Haran, and on the way, Jacob
had a dream. In Jacob's dream he saw a ladder stretching from
heaven to earth with angels. God promised to never leave
Jacob, to return him to his father's land, and to multiply his
descendants, as the dust of the earth is multiplied.

Jacob's ladder from God to man confirmed the promise that Jacob's lineage would yield the Messiah. Sometime
later God changed Jacob's name to Israel. God's plan was to
descend from heaven to bless the world through Israel. Jesus
is Jacob's ladder, the stairway to heaven.

Chenaniah

1 Chronicles {15:27} And David [was] clothed with a robe of fine linen, and all the Levites that bare the ark, and the singers, and Chenaniah the master of the song with the singers: David also [had] upon him an ephod of linen. {15:28} Thus all Israel brought up the ark of the covenant of the LORD with shouting, and with sound of the cornet, and with trumpets, and with cymbals, making a noise with psalteries and harps.

ANYONE WHO LOVES SINGING WILL LIKELY TELL YOU HOW wonderful singing makes them feel, how fun singing can be, and how singing brings people together.

Obed-edom was a man used by God to take care of the ark of the covenant after it was mishandled and people died. The ark was treated as holy under the care of Obed-edom and God greatly blessed him for it.

When David saw the blessing that the ark of the covenant brought, he respectfully sent for the ark to be brought back to its rightful place in Jerusalem. Upon the ark's return, David organized tens of thousands of men to worship God in song and Chenaniah had the great honor of leading the singing and music.

When times are good, it is easy to sing; however, we are also to sing when times seem sad. After the last supper, when Jesus was preparing to die for humanity, he sang. Like Chenaniah, Jesus led the music for the disciples, so to sing praises and worship God on the way to the cross.

The Centurion

Luke {23:47} Now when the centurion saw what was done, he glorified God, saying, Certainly this was a righteous man.

WHEN AN INNOCENT PERSON IS FALSELY ACCUSED THERE is a deep sense of distress. Most people will make every effort to clear their name from the false allegation or to defend themselves to prove their innocence.

The centurion, who guarded the foot of the cross of Jesus, saw the Jews' false charges against an innocent man and their mob to pressure for his crucifixion. The centurion saw Jesus gracefully accepting the torture and witnessed the kindness he showed to his mother. The centurion saw how Jesus prayed for forgiveness for the people who were mocking his cries of agony. The centurion saw how Jesus surrendered his life on the cross, and he observed supernatural events in his immediate surroundings with the darkened sun and the tearing of the temple veil.

Jesus made an impression on the centurion, and he continues to make an impression today. As a holy man, Jesus is the only one qualified to take the punishment of the sins of the world at the cross. Sin must be punished in death by God because he is holy. Jesus took on the penalty of sin at the cross and rose from the dead as a righteous King for all with faith in him. Out of love for humanity, Jesus willingly left heaven to live a life fit for the cross, so to impart his righteousness to sinners by faith. Has Jesus made an impression on you?

Chapter 8

—◆◆◆◆—

Psalm {90:2}
Before the mountains
were brought forth, or ever thou hadst
formed the earth and the world,
even from
everlasting to everlasting,
thou [art] God.

Pontius Pilate's Wife

Matthew {27:19} When he was set down on the judgment seat, his wife sent unto him, saying, Have thou nothing to do with that just man: for I have suffered many things this day in a dream because of him.

UNLESS YOU REALLY LOVE TO CLEAN, YOU LIKELY FIND IT discouraging how fast things get dirty. We live in a beautiful world that is full of physical and spiritual grime that requires constant cleansing.

Sin is like grime for our spirit, and it separates us from God. Since humans are born into a condition of spiritual sin there is a need for regular spiritual cleansing.

God used Pontius Pilate's wife to warn her husband that Jesus was sinless. Jesus was on trial before Pilate because the Jews were envious and outraged with Jesus's claim to be the Son of God and the king of the Jews. By posing Jesus as a political threat to Roman rule the Jews were seeking to eliminate Jesus to put an end to his authoritative teaching and popularity.

At the prompting of his wife, Pilate ceremonially removed himself from judgment on the holy man Jesus. Pilate publicly washed his hands of the matter with water and then used his authority to send Jesus to be crucified. Jesus washes our sins away in his precious blood that was shed at the cross, so we may put on his righteousness and stand before God with a clean heart forever.

The Azazel

Leviticus {16:22} And the goat shall bear upon him all their iniquities unto a land not inhabited: and he shall let go the goat in the wilderness.

PEOPLE LOSE SIGHT OF HOW MUCH THEY NEED JESUS; THEY fail God daily and feel guilty. It is easy to lose the feeling of joy when we dwell on our circumstances. How can we know the gladness of truth in a world full of sadness and confusion?

On the Day of Atonement, the high priest offered sacrifices for God's wrath for sin and for the removal of sin from himself and the people. Not only would God forgive the sin by accepting a burnt offering but he would demonstrate forgotten sin by using the Azazel to escape the guilt.

The Azazel was an actual "scapegoat" used ceremonially by the high priest to demonstrate how confessed sin is removed far away. God's people celebrated their gladness for forgiven and forgotten sin on this day each year. The undeserving animal bore the sins of the people for God and was released, carrying sin far away into the wilderness, also called the Azazel.

The gospel brings joy for believers willing to confess their sin and repent in Jesus's name. The Bible says that as far as the east is from the west, that is how far both sin and guilt have been removed from God's faithful. Glad are those who know that the Father sent the Son to be like the Azazel, to remove confessed sin and guilt from the sinner forever. Are you free from guilt?

Achsah

*Joshua {15:19} Who answered, Give me a blessing; for
thou hast given me a south land; give me also springs
of water. And he gave her the upper springs, and the
nether springs.*

WHAT A BLESSING IT IS TO PLAN FOR YOUR LOVED ONES
to receive an inheritance. Achsah's father Caleb was one of
the descendants to receive a portion of the promised land
that God promised to Abraham. Caleb entered the land and
possessed it as an inheritance from the Lord.

Caleb provided land as an inheritance for his daughter
Achsah, who intelligently saw that she needed springs of water
to secure her future livelihood there. Achsah had a kind and
generous father, whom she trusted, so she freely asked for
what she wanted without fear.

God the Father also has a sure inheritance secured for the
faithful, reserved according to the last will and testament of
the Lord Jesus Christ. The faithful are promised an inheritance of eternal life according to the scriptures. The Holy
Spirit is God's deposit in our hearts as proof.

Caleb planned an inheritance of land and springs for
Achsah and God the Father planned an inheritance for his
Son Jesus. Jesus's inheritance was from the beginning of time
and includes all believers that come to Jesus for forgiveness
of sins and eternal life. Not one of those destined to inherit
God's kingdom will be lost. Until the day we are face to face
with Jesus, let us continue to ask him for blessings freely and
bravely according to his will.

Haman

Esther {7:6} And Esther said, The adversary and enemy
[is] this wicked Haman. Then Haman was afraid
before the king and the queen.

THOSE WHO OPPOSE GOD'S WAYS OFTEN ALIGN THEMSELVES with people of power so to manipulate them into their illicit agenda. Haman opposed God and aligned himself with King Ahasuerus of Persia, whose queen was his beloved, Esther. Haman ordered that all would kneel and honor him and was furious at one Jewish man who refused. In revenge, Haman had the king sign a decree to kill this man and his people. Fifty-foot gallows were built to hang the man, Mordecai.

Haman's decree would take the life of the king's cherished queen. Haman relied on the law knowing that the king's decree was final and could not be overturned. The only person who had a chance to keep the lineage to God's anointed Messiah alive was Esther. Esther risked her life to host a banquet, to plead to the king for her life, and for the lives of her Jewish people.

The king signed a decree of grace to allow the Jews to defend themselves, and Haman, who opposed God and demanded honor, hung on his own gallows. The law could not be changed, so an alternate plan of grace was executed. Satan hopes in the law for humanity, so all will die forever in sin; however, God's alternate plan of grace was hidden in the mystery of scripture. Jesus is victorious over enemies like Haman by the cross because of God's grace for humanity.

The Olive Tree

Romans {11:19} Thou wilt say then, The branches were broken off, that I might be grafted in.

ONE DOES NOT HAVE TO BE A DOCTOR TO UNDERSTAND the helpful technique of grafting. When the damaged bone begs for secure stability, the idea of grafting is great. Grafting unites strong things to the weak, so to be stronger together.

Humans are not strangers to weakness. From the moment of birth, one cannot help but to be humbled by human dependence on stronger things needed for life. As people age, their sense of independence and pride creeps in. Pride tempts people to view themselves as self-sufficient.

Many people graft themselves onto their wealth, power, or status. Some arrogantly trust in their own goodness when the goodness of God is their only hope. The Jews failed when they rejected Jesus as their Messiah, so God rejected them and removed their prideful branches in God's olive tree. God used the weakness of Israel's failure to graft into God's family any non-Jew desiring strength in saving faith. The faithful are grafted into God's family by adoption.

The faithful grow their strength in the power of the Father by the anointing of the new covenant oil of the Spirit. One day the remnant of the chosen nation, Israel, will be grafted into God's olive tree once again, along with people groups from every nation in the world. Together weak, lost, sinful people will become strong because of the faithfulness of our great physician, the Messiah, The Lord and Savior, Jesus Christ.

Simon of Cyrene

Luke {23:26} And as they led him away, they laid hold upon one Simon, a Cyrenian, coming out of the country, and on him they laid the cross, that he might bear [it] after Jesus.

THERE ARE TIMES IN LIFE WHEN ONE RECOGNIZES THAT something incredibly painful must occur in order that the greater good will result. Giving birth, disciplining a wayward child, paying taxes, going for that mandatory medical procedure, and acquiring sore muscles from a workout are a few familiar examples of a necessary pain.

Simon of Cyrene was a foreigner God used to bless Jesus during a necessary time of suffering for the sins of the world. Jesus was wounded beyond recognition and forced to carry the cross to be crucified; however, due to the physical condition, Jesus was unable, so Simon met the need.

Simon of Cyrene was forced to carry Jesus's cross. Simon of Cyrene was a necessary help to Jesus as he faced torturous death. Christians are called to bear their cross and follow Jesus, and this requires a commitment to obey at random times, no matter the cost, convenience, or desirability.

Simon of Cyrene witnessed and participated in God's plan from eternity as it unfolded. The cross is a bittersweet reminder of God's love. The innocent had to die for the guilty, or everyone would die. From eternity, Jesus agreed that agony would be worth the pain for the greater good.

Bezalel

Exodus {35:30} And Moses said unto the children of
Israel, See, the LORD hath called by name Bezaleel
the son of Uri, the son of Hur, of the tribe of Judah;
{35:31} And he hath filled him with the spirit of God,
in wisdom, in understanding, and in knowledge,
and in all manner of workmanship.

WHEN ADAM AND EVE WERE CREATED IT WAS CLEAR THAT
God wanted a place of beauty to dwell with them, right in
the garden of Eden. When the fellowship was broken due to
sin, God revealed a continued desire to dwell with people;
however, there would be conditions.

God desired to dwell with his people in the traveling
tabernacle; however, to accomplish this fellowship the priests
had to make atonement for their own sins, and for the sins of
the people, at the mercy seat. The temporary place of meeting
was created to be especially beautiful, and God chose a special
man to create a glorious masterpiece.

The Holy Spirit helped Bezalel to create, and teach others
to labor in love, a masterpiece dwelling place, a tabernacle
suitable for the Creator of the universe. Bezalel designed the
temple; the ark of the covenant; the mercy seat; the table; the
lampstands; the altar of incense; the altar of burnt offering;
basin of bronze; and the ornate, golden, beautiful fixtures
for God's temple.

Jesus's finished work on the cross has also created a new
dwelling place. Your heart is God's masterpiece tabernacle.
Does the Holy Spirit dwell with you everywhere you go?

The Garden of Eden

Genesis {2:15} And the LORD God took the man, and put him into the garden of Eden to dress it and to keep it.

PEOPLE HAVE A NATURAL INCLINATION TO DESIRE A BETTER place because God has placed eternity in their hearts. God could have placed Adam and Eve in any random place; however, paradise was the best choice, in the garden of Eden.

The garden of Eden was a paradise complete with every animal, plant, and opportunity to freely go about life in the presence of God's glory. Free will requires choice, so God placed one forbidden tree in the garden, "the tree of the knowledge of good and evil." If people did not eat from the forbidden tree they could freely eat from the "tree of life" and live forever with God.

Free will for humanity is necessary for God's glory. Any friend or loved one knows that a forced friendship is never enjoyed. Friendships are sweet when there is reciprocity and sincerity.

Scripture says that no eye has seen, nor ear heard, nor has the human heart come close to imagining the wonderfulness that God has planned for those who love Jesus. Eden's garden was just a glimpse of the goodness of God and the glory that he desires to share with us in righteousness forever.

Revelation {22:3} And there shall be no more curse: but the throne of God and of the Lamb shall be in it; and his servants shall serve him: {22:4} And they shall see his face; and his name [shall be] in their foreheads.

Saul

Jeremiah {17:9} The heart [is] deceitful above all
[things,] and desperately wicked: who can know it?

THE GENERAL DIRECTION OF ORDER IN THE WORLD SEEMS
to be new birth, when all is well, followed by decline and
eventual death. Human beings are best at failing when left to
depend on their own free will apart from God.

Once Israel conquered some of its promised land, its
people lived and functioned independently as twelve tribes,
and they did whatever seemed right according to their conscience. God's chosen people were not satisfied to live depend-
ing on God alone. Israel wanted a king to rule over them like
the surrounding nations had, despite the warning that came
from the prophet Samuel.

God gave Saul as king, and he started off well. Saul enjoyed
God-given victories in battle; however, he became prideful. Saul
followed his own deceitful heart by stealing from and lying to
God, so God took the Holy Spirit away. When Saul realized
that God was with David, he was determined to kill David.
Saul made many mistakes and David could have killed him.
David was faithful to preserve Saul's life, time and time again.

King Saul's life reminds how easy it is to succumb to the
general direction of order, when things seem new and well,
only to realize sin's influence that leads to decline and death.
King Jesus's life reminds how God has put an end to the world
order of decline and death with the righteous life and resurrection of his Son. The faithful are promised that the Holy
Spirit will never leave them, so their life may become new and
well forever in the spiritual kingdom of heaven.

Leah

Genesis {29:31} And when the LORD saw that Leah [was] hated, he opened her womb.

GOD HAS A PLAN FOR EACH ONE OF US, REGARDLESS OF IF we feel beautiful or not. Leah was a woman whom the Bible describes as homely, her younger sister Rachel was beautiful.

The custom for marriage required that the older daughters be married before the younger daughters. Rachel was in love and wanted to be married first, so Jacob agreed to labor for seven years for Rachel's hand.

The morning after the wedding Jacob discovered that he was tricked into marrying Leah, per the custom. Leah's father made another agreement with Jacob. Jacob could also marry Rachel if he agreed to stay and labor for another seven years. Leah's husband, Jacob, married her sister Rachel seven days after their wedding celebration. Jacob loved Rachel more than Leah. Leah felt loathed by her sister and husband. God saw Leah's heartbreak and loved her.

God had a plan for Leah to feel the beauty and love of motherhood. God used Leah in the plan of salvation. Leah's son Levi became the line of the family of Israel chosen to be the priests of God. The Levites would be the only ones to serve as priests in the tabernacle and in the temple of the Lord. Leah's son Judah became the one whom God used to carry out the promise to Jacob's grandfather Abraham. Through Leah, her son Judah's descendants would yield the Messiah, the Lord Jesus.

Eliezer

2 Timothy {1:7} For God hath not given us the spirit of fear; but of power, and of love, and of a sound mind.

ELIEZER WAS HEAD SERVANT TO HIS MASTER ABRAHAM. Eliezer's master made him swear an oath to not let his master's son marry a woman of the Canaanites, in the region where they lived. Abraham wanted a virtuous woman to marry his son, from his homeland in the region of Mesopotamia.

Genesis 24 reveals how Eliezer obediently did the will of his master, though afraid no woman would go with him. Eliezer prayed that God would make it clear who his master's son's bride would be based on her generous nature, and as he prayed the woman Rebekah appeared. Eliezer told the family all that his master had told him. The family agreed that it was God's will for Rebekah to go.

Eliezer trusted that God answered his prayer by directing him to the house of his master's kinsmen and locating Rebekah. Eliezer shared the message of his master to the family of the bride-to-be, revealing every detail out of his love for his master. Eliezer put his master's will before any other.

Eliezer was an exemplary servant; however, Jesus is the supreme servant. Jesus left paradise to become an obedient man, to teach us how to live, and to put the will of the Father before his own will. Jesus trusted in God and went to the cross to take our place of punishment for sin. May we be faithful servants and live for Jesus.

Mephibosheth

*2 Samuel {9:6} Now when Mephibosheth, the son of
Jonathan, the son of Saul, was come unto David, he
fell on his face, and did reverence. And David said,
Mephibosheth. And he answered, Behold thy servant!
{9:7} And David said unto him, Fear not: for I will
surely shew thee kindness for Jonathan thy father's sake,
and will restore thee all the land of Saul thy father; and
thou shalt eat bread at my table continually.*

OCCASIONALLY, WE ARE ASKED TO MAKE A PROMISE WITH
someone who trusts us to keep our word. Promises give
people hope. Promises are especially important in scripture
and God expects his people to keep their word when they
make a promise.

When King Saul's rule over Israel ended it was time for
David to take his rightful place as the anointed king of Israel.
It was typical for a new dynasty to destroy the descendants
of the old dynasty during this transition. Saul's son Jonathan
and David shared a mutual friendship of love. Both Saul and
Jonathan asked David to promise that he would not destroy
their descendants and David kept his word.

Jonathan's son Mephibosheth was spared a life of fear
because David kept his promise. Believers are spared the
fear of eternal death because Jesus kept his promise. Out of
kindness, the Father promised to send the Son. Jesus faced
the fear of the cross, so the faithful would be restored to God,
and not destroyed. Believers look forward to eating bread at
the Lord's table continually.

Boaz

*Ruth {3:9} And he said, Who [art] thou? And she
answered, I [am] Ruth thine handmaid: spread
therefore thy skirt over thine handmaid; for thou
[art] a near kinsman.*

A BEAUTIFUL MOABITE WIDOW, BY THE NAME OF RUTH,
followed her mother-in-law, Naomi, to her homeland in
Bethlehem, where a love story would change her life forever.

Boaz was a wise, kind, and wealthy landowner who was
a relative to Ruth's deceased husband. Boaz noticed Ruth
gleaning the fields and told her to stay close to his land and
his women who were working. Boaz offered Ruth to eat with
his women, ordered his men to provide her security, and commanded his workers to leave extra bundles of grain for her.
Boaz was so kind because he learned that Ruth was a worthy
and virtuous woman.

Naomi, being familiar with the custom of her people,
knew that Ruth could be redeemed by a willing relative, a
kinsman redeemer, and Boaz was second in line to redeem
Ruth as his wife. Following her mother-in-law's instruction,
Ruth laid at the feet of sleeping Boaz.

Immediately, Boaz made the legal and proper arrangements to redeem Ruth as his own. God blessed Ruth and she
conceived a son, Obed, the great grandfather of King David.
From the family line of Boaz came the lineage to our Lord
and Savior, Jesus Christ.

The Bible is the greatest love story ever told. Jesus is our
perfect kinsman redeemer who makes people worthy and
virtuous by his righteous life, given at the cross.

Joab

Matthew {25:21} His lord said unto him, Well done, [thou] good and faithful servant: thou hast been faithful over a few things, I will make thee ruler over many things: enter thou into the joy of thy lord.

EXPERIENCING THE SATISFYING REWARD OF A JOB WELL done does not just happen randomly. Strategy must be implemented and followed through to realize success.

There are two quite different worldviews to consider when contemplating strategy for success. The secular worldview often pursues a goal with the idea that the ends justify the means. The Christian worldview has a common goal to serve God by faithfully doing his will.

Joab was a shrewd servant to King David and a warrior. Joab often placed his will above his master's will for his own gain, his goal strategy was not as important as his success. Joab took advantage for revenge and committed murder during a time of peace, causing King David trouble. Joab was responsible for the death of David's son Absalom. Joab tried to remove the kingdom from David's son Solomon, so to be received well by the new administration.

Joab was shrewd in a manner that he thought would lead to his honor; however, he died poorly. Jesus offers a strategy for the reward for a job well done. Jesus teaches the faithful to be shrewd in a God-honoring manner. When we faithfully and obediently follow Jesus in all things, by the power of the Holy Spirit, we have hope to joyfully receive eternal rewards in heaven.

Chapter 9

2 Corinthians {3:12}
Seeing then that
we have such hope,
we use great
plainness of speech.

Potiphar's Wife

Proverbs {20:6} Most men will proclaim every one his own goodness: but a faithful man who can find?

SOME PEOPLE LACK CONTENTMENT, THEY WANT THEIR latest heart's desire regardless of who they hurt.

Joseph was Jacob's eleventh son and the favorite. Joseph's brothers were jealous, so they sold him to Egypt. Joseph became a stranger in a strange land where he was expected to be contented to serve. Joseph did serve, trusting in the faithfulness of God.

Potiphar purchased Joseph to be his servant. Potiphar's wife noticed how handsome Joseph was, and she made him her latest heart's desire. When Joseph was alone, Potiphar's wife advanced. Joseph refused to sin against Potiphar and against God, so he fled. Potiphar's wife tore Joseph's garment as he ran away and used it as evidence of an attempted assault to send him to prison.

Joseph suffered for a crime that he did not commit because this was part of God's plan of redemption. Potiphar's wife, like the enemy of God, is a tempter, liar, and accuser. Jesus too was falsely accused by an enemy and he suffered for sins that he did not commit because this too was part of God's plan of redemption.

Our lack of contentment in God's perfect plan opens the door to our temptation to sin, and our unfaithfulness grieves the Spirit. Even so, God loves us so much that he sent us Jesus to be a suffering servant, to cover our sins by his righteous life, death, and resurrection. May we crave contentment in the faithfulness of Jesus. What is your heart's desire?

The Young Man of Egypt

1 Samuel {30:15} And David said to him, Canst thou bring me down to this company? And he said, Swear unto me by God, that thou wilt neither kill me, nor deliver me into the hands of my master, and I will bring thee down to this company.

UPON RETURN FROM A BATTLE, DAVID FOUND HIS CAMP burned, with the wives, families, and treasures stolen by the Amalekites. David and his men grieved until David found strength in the Lord to inquire of the priest what to do. God told David to take his men to go rescue all that was lost.

Six hundred men deployed with David, but the journey was hard. Along the way God inserted a desperate man who needed help, one to help David find the stolen treasures. The young man of Egypt was weak, left behind from his service by those responsible for David's loss.

The young man of Egypt accepted David's help and trusted his oath, sworn to him by God. The young man led David to his possessions where they battled fiercely, rescued the wives and families, and restored their treasures. David honored his word and shared treasures with the young man.

Like the young man of Egypt trusted David, we can trust Jesus because Jesus kept his oath from creation. Jesus left heaven, became a man, battled temptation, went to the cross, defeated death, rescued God's treasured family, and restored to God all that was stolen in the garden of Eden.

Malchus

John {18:10} Then Simon Peter having a sword drew it, and smote the high priest's servant, and cut off his right ear. The servant's name was Malchus.

INTELLIGENT PEOPLE RECOGNIZE WHEN ACTION MUST BE executed. Malchus was a servant of a high priest who was doing his job when the warrant for Jesus's arrest was issued.

Malchus dodged a sword to his head and suffered the loss of his ear, then he received unmerited healing from the one he was to arrest. After falling back from Jesus's powerful declaration of identity, and then being healed by Jesus, it is likely Malchus was filled with awe.

Malchus set aside his wonder and responded with intelligent action when it was time to execute the order to arrest Jesus. Malchus was the last person recorded in scripture to receive miraculous physical healing from the Lord Jesus during the earthly ministry.

Jesus's earthly mission ended, so that victory over the grave would be achieved through precious blood that was shed at the cross. By the power of the Holy Spirit, Jesus was declared holy and resurrected from the grave, so he may reconcile sinful humanity to God the Father.

One sweet day, King Jesus will return to heal his people. May God's faithful execute their lives intelligently, and act obediently, so to be found faithful upon his return. God's desire is to share the glory of Jesus with all whom the Father has given him from eternity, not one will be lost.

Priscilla

Acts {18:26} And he began to speak boldly in the synagogue: whom when Aquila and Priscilla had heard, they took him unto [them,] and expounded unto him the way of god more perfectly.

PRISCILLA WAS THE WIFE OF AQUILA; BOTH WERE TENT makers who fled Rome because of Jewish persecution. Priscilla learned from the Apostle Paul the true significance of the death and resurrection of the Lord Jesus Christ. Priscilla was gracious, hospitable, and helpful in ministry.

Apollos came to town to teach about Jesus; however, Priscilla recognized that he needed help. Apollos was missing an especially important piece of the mystery of what God had planned for the church. God planned to include all nations, not just the Jews. Priscilla knew that Apollos had to understand that the baptism of the Holy Spirit was superior to the baptism of John the Baptist.

The baptism of John was a symbolic water cleansing for the Jews who were looking for their Messiah. The baptism of the Holy Spirit is superior to the baptism of John because it is a spiritual cleansing and empowering work performed by God because of Jesus's finished work at the cross. The baptism of the Holy Spirit produces a new spiritual birth to eternal life.

The baptism of the Holy Spirit joins people together who are otherwise separated by boundaries of social class and ethnicity. For this reason, Priscilla, a woman during a time when women were regarded as inferior to men, felt confident to help teach alongside of her husband.

Shaphan

2 Kings {22:10} And Shaphan the scribe shewed the king, saying, Hilkiah the priest hath delivered me a book. And Shaphan read it before the king.

THERE IS NO QUESTION THAT EVERY HOME OR OFFICE WITH a good secretary effectively managing the day-to-day operation will do well.

Shaphan was the secretary to one of the youngest kings of Judah who began to reign at the age of eight. King Josiah desired to do good for the Lord; however, he had no understanding of God's law. Shaphan's king ordered a restoration of the temple of the Lord, with strict orders concerning payment to the workers. Shaphan followed orders well.

Shaphan was advised by Hilkiah, the priest, that the book of the law was discovered, so he read the words to King Josiah. God's wrath was kindled against the people because they did not honor God's law. The young king sent for a message from the Lord to help him understand what the words in the book meant for the people and for all of Judah.

Shaphan's ability to recognize God's law changed the life of King Josiah. King Josiah obeyed the book of the law and lived a life that was devoted to the Lord. Like Shaphan, believers will do well to read the book of the law for understanding, so to confidently share the gospel with others.

Like Shaphan helped Josiah, Jesus helps believers to manage the day-to-day operations of life. There is no better restoration for humanity than to follow the Bible in obedience to God's will.

Absalom

2 Samuel {14:25} But in all Israel there was none to be so much praised as Absalom for his beauty: from the sole of his foot even to the crown of his head there was no blemish in him.

SOME PEOPLE ARE SIMPLY UNWILLING TO SUBMIT TO authority. Many people want to be their own lord and make decisions as they wish, regardless of temporal or eternal consequences.

Absalom was King David's beloved, beautiful son. Absalom lost respect for his father as he matured, he lacked trust in judgment and justice from the throne.

Absalom committed evil against his father, King David, and fled the kingdom. Absalom went so far as to declare himself king, instructing his men to hunt and kill his father, King David; however, God spoiled their plan.

In his failure to overthrow his father, Absalom was murdered by one of his father's men, causing his father, King David, unbearable grief. King David loved his son Absalom with an unbreakable bond of emotion, but Absalom did not reciprocate his father's feelings.

By great love and for his glory, God created his first unblemished, beautiful man, Adam. God gave Adam free will to trust in him and enjoy loving reciprocity, or to not trust him.

May believers with wayward children find comfort remembering that God, who is the perfect parent, his first man, Adam, refused to trust him. Jesus is the beloved, beautiful Son of God whom the Father sent, so we may trust his perfect judgment and justice from his eternal throne.

Golgotha

John {19:16} Then delivered he him therefore unto them to be crucified. And they took Jesus, and led [him] away. {19:17} And he bearing his cross went forth into a place called [the place] of a skull, which is called in the Hebrew Golgotha: {19:18} Where they crucified him, and two others with him, on either side one, and Jesus in the midst.

FOR MOST OF THE EARTH'S POPULATION, THERE IS AN awareness of extremes. One is either rich or poor, intelligent or ignorant, healthy or sick, clean or dirty, innocent or guilty, and more. Rarely will one have just enough of anything to truly be satisfied. Humanitarians seek to bridge the divide.

A set of extremes were present at the cross at Golgotha. Golgotha was set high on a hill, so that all could see the wrath of Rome's crucifixion punishment for their most wicked criminals. High on a hill, Jesus's innocent body hanged between two guilty criminals as an extreme ransom.

At Golgotha, God demonstrated his desire to bridge the divide between his holiness and personal sin. Sinful people may inherit righteousness while acting in their own free will because of the person and work of Jesus.

The cross on the hill at Golgotha absorbed the blood that cries out to God's people to choose their extreme. Death or life, war or peace, hate or love, blame or forgiveness, ruin or restoration, judgment or redemption, belief or unbelief, to be saved or condemned for eternity. Golgotha raises awareness for your extreme. What is your choice?

The Thankful Leper

Luke {17:16} And fell down on [his] face at his feet,
giving him thanks: and he was a Samaritan.
{17:17} And Jesus answering said, Were there not ten
cleansed? but where [are] the nine?

SHOWING GRATITUDE IS ONE OF THE SIMPLEST, MOST POW-erful ways to give an acknowledgment to someone you value. Most people appreciate appreciative people, and so does God.

In Jesus's time, leprosy was a common disease. Once diagnosed by the priest, lepers would never be allowed to be with their families again, unless they were healed, and the priest declared them to be clean. Lepers were regarded as physically and spiritually unclean.

As Jesus was teaching and performing signs and miracles, ten hopeful lepers called out for help. Jesus was compassionate and healed them all; however, only one returned to give thanks. The thankful leper truly appreciated his gift of healing, he could now be reconciled to his community.

Leprosy was serious because it separated people from each other, but sin is even more serious. Sin is so repulsive that all who die in their sin will be eternally separated from the God of the Bible, without hope. Praise the Lord for making a way for sinful people to be reunited with God through the person and work of Jesus Christ in the power of the Holy Spirit.

Scripture says that every perfect gift is from the heavenly Father, and he appreciates appreciative people. Believers must never forget to give thanks for every good gift and every trial we may face in God's grace.

Hur

Exodus {17:12} But Moses' hands [were] heavy; and they took a stone, and put [it] under him, and he sat thereon; and Aaron and Hur stayed up his hands, the one on the one side, and the other on the other side; and his hands were steady until the going down of the sun.

HUR WAS A HELPER WHO LEFT HIS MARK IN THE PAGES OF scripture. As the Israelites were vulnerable and learning to trust God for all their provisions in the desert, they were attacked. Moses acted with a plan for God's glory and sent Joshua to fight.

Moses, his brother Aaron, and Hur all went together high on a hilltop. Moses held his staff high in the air from the top of the hill to encourage Joshua in battle. When Moses's staff was lowered the men failed and when his staff was raised the men prevailed. Moses needed help to hold up his arms to raise the staff high, so Hur and Aaron held his arms as God worked to deliver the Israelites to victory. The fighting men took heart in looking up to the hill and seeing strength.

God has a plan for both leaders and helpers. Without helpers like Hur, leaders like Moses would fail. God values every person in his family, and none are of more value than another.

Leaders and helpers are called to share the gospel to grow God's kingdom. When you feel weak remember that it is okay to ask your friends, brothers, and Jesus for help. May the Holy Spirit be the helper who leaves his mark in the pages of your heart. *Romans {8:26} Likewise the Spirit also helpeth our infirmities.*

Jabez

1 Chronicles {4:10} And Jabez called on the God of Israel, saying, Oh that thou wouldest bless me indeed, and enlarge my coast, and that thine hand might be with me, and that thou wouldest keep [me] from evil, that it may not grieve me! And God granted him that which he requested.

MANY PEOPLE STRUGGLE WITH PRAYER, EVEN PEOPLE WHO have great faith. God wants people to pray in thankfulness and make all their requests known.

Jabez was a descendant of Judah, as was the Lord Jesus. Jabez was an honorable man who believed in God's promises to prosper the nation of Israel. Jabez believed in the power of prayer.

Jabez's life began as a source of pain and sorrow, yet he trusted God. Jabez confidently and with humility prayed for a blessing trusting in God's faithfulness and will.

In Matthew 6:9, Jesus taught a divine outline on how to pray for God's will effectively. The Lord's prayer is not a repetitious prayer but an outline that is personal between the believer and God. When we pray this way, we worship God's holy name, we look forward to heaven, we desire God's will, we are satisfied, we seek forgiveness, we forgive others, and pursue eternal holiness.

Praying for God's will, in the power of the Holy Spirit, using scripture as an outline, is a wonderful way to keep prayers fresh. Do you pray for God's will? Go ahead, give God thanks, pray confidently, pray continually, and pray like Jabez, with humility and trust in God's will.

Rhoda

Acts {12:13} And as Peter knocked at the door of the gate, a damsel came to hearken, named Rhoda. {12:14} And when she knew Peter's voice, she opened not the gate for gladness, but ran in, and told how Peter stood before the gate.

SCRIPTURE TEACHES THAT IT IS IMPOSSIBLE TO PLEASE God without faith. Rhoda was a servant girl who had faith. The disciples were praying in earnest for Peter in Rhoda's master's home because Peter was imprisoned by Herod.

An angel of the Lord appeared to Peter in prison, just before Herod was to take him away, and Peter's chains fell off his hands. Peter got dressed and followed the angel out of the jail and through the iron gate of the prison that opened on its own accord. Peter was free.

When Peter arrived at Rhoda's master's gate and knocked, the disciples did not believe Rhoda. Rhoda did believe that God had answered the prayers of the disciples and that Peter was free. Rhoda's confidence was in stark contrast to the disciples who were praying and not believing. The disciples went as far as to call Rhoda "crazy" for thinking that God answered their prayers.

When everything in the world seems to be at odds against you, remember that we serve a mighty Savior. Our Father hears, sees, and answers prayers when we pray for God's will and glory in the name of Jesus. Ask the Holy Spirit to increase your faith. With God, all things are possible.

Jethro

Exodus {18:6} And he said unto Moses, I thy father in law Jethro am come unto thee, and thy wife, and her two sons with her.

WHAT IS THE DIFFERENCE BETWEEN A FINE LAWYER AND the finest lawyer? A fine lawyer knows every detail of the law. The finest lawyer knows every detail of the law and is a friend with the judge.

Moses was chosen to give the Israelites the laws that God would have them obey. Moses was also chosen to monitor the affairs of God's people to ensure that disputes were settled peacefully according to God's law. God's people had gained in number significantly in Egypt. Moses was the only one who heard the disputes of all of God's people from morning until night.

Jethro was the priest of Midian and the father-in-law of Moses. When Jethro delivered Moses's wife and children into his care, he made a significant observation and offered advice. Jethro advised Moses to train others to learn every detail of the law, so to fairly judge the people because the task was too great for one man.

Moses was a friend to the finest, most important, trustworthy judge of all, the God of the universe. Jethro recognized the need for a judge that would never tire out. Jesus is the finest giver of the law, and eternal judge, who will never tire out. Someday in God's honest court every knee will bow, and every tongue confess that Jesus Christ is Lord to the glory of God.

Nicodemus

*John {3:4} Nicodemus saith unto him, How can a man
be born when he is old? Can he enter the second time
into his mother's womb, and be born?*

THERE ARE TWO THINGS SO STRONGLY ASSOCIATED THAT
do not exist apart, they are learning and teaching.

Nicodemus was a teacher to Israel who had a lot to learn
about Jesus. When Nicodemus felt safe, at night and in secret,
he went to the source of all knowledge to learn all that he
needed to know.

Jesus explained to Nicodemus that the Jews were seeking an earthly king for Israel. Jesus taught that he is Israel's
true king in a spiritual kingdom for all eternity. Nicodemus
learned that the Son of God had to descend from heaven, so
to be lifted on the cross, die, and be resurrected, so all who
believe would be given eternal life in Jesus's name.

Since God's kingdom is spiritual and eternal, it cannot
be inherited by flesh and blood because humanity is sinful
and will die. Humans need to inherit eternal life to enter the
spiritual, eternal kingdom of God, and this requires a new
spiritual birth of the heart. People are born again when they
receive spiritual life in Jesus's name.

God gives believers the Holy Spirit to dwell in their hearts
forever, and this new spiritual birth must occur before the
natural man dies. Jesus provides a spiritual transformation
that can come only from God above. Life eternal is given as
a gift to the believer who asks for faith in Jesus.

The Man with an Unclean Spirit

Luke {4:33} And in the synagogue there was a man,
which had a spirit of an unclean devil, and cried out
with a loud voice.

THE IMAGINATION OF GOD'S CHOSEN PEOPLE PROMOTED customs above and beyond the laws given by Moses. By requiring God's people to meet imaginative standards of holiness, the stage was set for Jesus to make enemies of the Jewish leaders by performing good works on the Sabbath.

The man with an unclean spirit was in the synagogue one Sabbath as Jesus was teaching. Suddenly the unclean spirits within the man viciously accused Jesus personally. Jesus commanded the unclean spirits to come out of the man and they did so without harm. The man with an unclean spirit likely never imagined that he would be healed by Jesus in the synagogue on the Sabbath.

The works and miracles that Jesus did are worthy of the use of one's imagination. Imagine the number of sick people of all ages who sought out Jesus. Imagine the number of those healed from the unclean spirits. Imagine Jesus's love, as he accomplished his mission with precious blood shed at the cross, so that God's faithful may escape evil and have eternal life. How wonderful to have an imagination to consider the great love of Jesus.

John {21:25} And there are also many other things which
Jesus did, the which, if they should be written every one, I sup-
pose that even the world itself could not contain the books that
should be written.

Chapter 10

Isaiah {12:4}
And in that day shall ye say,
Praise the LORD, call upon his name,
declare his doings among the people,
make mention that his name is exalted.

Jemima

Job {42:14} And he called the name of the first, Jemima; and the name of the second, Kezia; and the name of the third, Keren-happuch. {42:15} And in all the land were no women found [so] fair as the daughters of Job: and their father gave them inheritance among their brethren.

SOMETIMES SAD THINGS HAPPEN TO FAITHFUL PEOPLE, BUT we still trust in God's wisdom.

Jemima's father, Job, was a man of great faith in God, who experienced great blessings from God. Satan approached God concerning Jemima's father, advising that if he lost his wealth, health, and happiness, he would curse God. God knew that Satan was wrong, so God allowed Jemima's father to suffer for a time at the hand of the enemy, but God guaranteed his life.

Jemima's father lost his wealth, health, and happiness. Jemima's father became sick and poor, and his children died. Jemima's father was told by his wife to curse God and die; however, he remained faithful. After a time, God proved his faithfulness to Jemima's father and restored him to an even greater measure of life's blessings than he experienced prior to his losses. Jemima's father lived to enjoy his days for four additional generations.

Jemima had a faithful and generous father who endured trials and was sure to give his beautiful daughters an inheritance out of his great love for them.

Jesus also has a faithful and generous Father who endured trials and is sure to give his beautiful church an inheritance, out of his great love for them.

Jehoahaz

2 Kings {13:4} And Jehoahaz besought the LORD, and the LORD hearkened unto him: for he saw the oppression of Israel, because the king of Syria oppressed them. {13:5} (And the LORD gave Israel a saviour.

HUMANITY IS LOST WITHOUT GOD'S SAVIOR, JESUS. WHEN people are caught up in their delight for sin, they often feel God's judgment and discipline. When God punishes his people, they tend to call out to God to save them. Once things are well again, some people who benefit from God's goodness will forget God and his savior and reveal their true colors by their delight in sin.

Jehoahaz was a king who longed for both a savior and a lifestyle of sin. Jehoahaz caused Israel to sin, so God became angry and judged his people by allowing their oppression by the enemy. Jehoahaz sought the Lord to save them. God graciously listened to Jehoahaz's desire for the favor of the Lord, and then mercifully sent a savior to protect Israel in order that the people may remain safe in their homes.

Like many people, Jehoahaz displayed his true colors as he turned his back on God and once again led the Israelites to worship idols and offend God.

The Savior that God gave to humanity does not grant a pass to sin; he desires loyalty to righteousness. Jesus knows that believers' hearts are like Jehoahaz and are prone to turn away. The Holy Spirit transforms believers to be like Jesus, so they will not be content to delight in sin.

The Bible

2 Timothy {3:16} All scripture [is] given by inspiration of God, and [is] profitable for doctrine, for reproof, for correction, for instruction in righteousness.

THE MARKS OF A GOOD READ ARE EASY TO RECOGNIZE. There is a powerful launch, telling an irresistible story with convincing persons, all while offering unique design and discourse.

There is no other book that comes close to all that the Bible offers. There is no other book that makes the bold claim that God is the author. The Bible claims to be the full authority of God, in sixty-six different books, penned by almost forty human authors, all inspired by the Holy Spirit. The Bible is the only book ever to be repeatedly targeted for annihilation.

The Bible was written over a span of approximately two thousand years, on three continents, and in three different languages. The Bible reveals God's historical narrative of Israel. The Bible is full of fulfilled prophecy of both Jesus's first and second coming.

The Bible possesses the attributes of God—never changing, always true, independent—and is the source of all wisdom and understanding. The Bible reveals God's fury at sin, his love for humanity, and Jesus's imminent return.

There is no denying the uniqueness of literary styles in scripture, the clarity of the person and work of Jesus, and the unapologetic, historical accuracy when compared against science and archaeology. Genesis 1:1 is the basis for scientific study, introducing elements that cannot exist independently—time, space, and matter. In the beginning, God created the heavens and the earth.

The Man with a Withered Hand

*Luke {6:6} And it came to pass also on another sabbath,
that he entered into the synagogue and taught: and
there was a man whose right hand was withered.*

ALTHOUGH THE GOODNESS OF GOD IS ALWAYS EVERY-where, there is something special about the sanctuary. In the temple, church, or synagogue, God's faithful sense God through faith, hope, and love. Unfortunately, in many houses of worship, the leaders have altered the direction of worship to honor man-made traditions above and beyond God's will.

While Jesus was living among his possession Israel, to reveal to the people their promised redemption, the Jewish leaders were pressured to follow man-made traditions. The law of Moses was intended to mandate God's people to love and help each other. Unfortunately, Israelite leaders favored their man-made tradition to not do any work on the Sabbath. Performing a good work for God was forbidden, exposing their Sabbath as being treated like an idol.

The man with a withered hand was likely there in the synagogue longing for Jesus to expose God's goodness. Jesus did just that by healing his hand on the Sabbath. Jesus showed this man love by making him an example of the most important commandment, to love God and neighbor.

May believers around the world evaluate their own traditions and decide if they are truly God-honoring based on the source of the Bible. Traditions can be lovely; however, when the tradition is more important than God's will, then glory is shifted from the Creator to the created.

Mordecai

Esther {4:13} Then Mordecai commanded to answer Esther, Think not with thyself that thou shalt escape in the king's house, more than all the Jews.

IT IS IMPORTANT TO DEMONSTRATE LOYALTY WITH ACTION, yet some believers prefer to lay low and keep their faith private for fear of rejection by unbelievers.

Mordecai was a Jew whose lineage was from the tribe of Benjamin, who lived in Persia after the Babylonians carried off God's nation Israel into captivity. Mordecai took in and cared for his beautiful niece Esther, who was an orphan. King Ahasuerus removed his wife Queen Vashti and sought out a new queen from the citadel of Susa. After a year of purification, Esther was chosen and crowned queen; however, she followed Mordecai's instruction to keep her faith private.

Mordecai overheard a plot to have the Jewish people destroyed, thus putting the lineage to the Savior in jeopardy. Mordecai advised his niece Esther to approach the king and plead for her people. This task was difficult because no one could approach the king and live unless he granted a pardon. Mordecai urged Esther to be loyal.

Mordecai commanded Esther to demonstrate her loyalty to God with action by going public with her Jewish faith. Esther did bring the message to the king and as a result the Jews lived. Jesus also acted and went public with his identity when it was time to face the horror of the cross, which was necessary so that the faithful would live. Jesus pardons sin and desires public loyalty.

The Visions and Dreams

Numbers {12:7} My servant Moses [is] not so,
who [is] faithful in all mine house.
{12:8} With him will I speak mouth to mouth,
even apparently, and not in dark speeches.

SOMETIMES PEOPLE DESIRE MYSTERIOUS SPIRITUAL EXPE-
riences. It seems like it would be comforting to have a private
word from God. Wishing for a vision or a dream with a message from God is common. Listening for God's will should
be the aim of the faithful.

God spoke to individuals by visions as recorded in scripture. Jacob, also named Israel, had a vision concerning God's
promises for him. Samuel had visions of God's future for the
people. Both Peter's and Cornelius's visions revealed God's
ultimate plan for salvation beyond Israel.

God used a dream to offer King Solomon any wish he
would ask for under the sun. God gave Daniel the ability to
interpret dreams for kings like Nebuchadnezzar and Belshazzar in addition to visions of events yet to come. God comforted Joseph's nerves in a dream after learning that Mary was
expecting baby Jesus prior to marriage. God granted visions
and dreams to some, but Moses was different. God spoke to
Moses, mouth to mouth.

Receiving a message by visions or dreams may seem desirable; however, this pales in comparison to receiving messages
mouth to mouth. 2 Corinthians 11:14 says that Satan disguises
himself as an angel of light, so beware of mysterious messages.
Moses was different and so are we. The faithful hear from Jesus,
mouth to mouth, by the words in the precious Holy Bible.

Jael

*Judges {5:24} Blessed above women shall Jael the wife of
Heber the Kenite be, blessed shall she be above women
in the tent. {5:26} She put her hand to the nail, and
her right hand to the workmen's hammer; and with the
hammer she smote Sisera.*

SIN WOULD CYCLE THROUGH THE GENERATIONS FROM TIME
to time. Israel spent a great deal of time in a state of war or
captivity because of its repeated sin cycle.

The Israelites loved their sin, so God sold them to King
Jabin of Canaan. God's people were oppressed cruelly for
twenty years before they cried to God for help. Israel needed to
battle the king and his army commander, Sisera. When Sisera
learned that the Israelites were ready for battle, he fled to the
home of Heber, where he felt safe, and was welcomed by Jael.

God used Jael, a woman, to triumph over Sisera. Jael recognized the need to remove this adversary to live peacefully.
Jael was willing to go to an extreme, so she drove a tent peg
into his head. The Israelites killed the king of Canaan and
lived for the Lord in peace for forty years.

Jesus was willing to go to the extreme of the cross to battle
the death effect of the sin cycle. Matthew 5:29-30 teaches that
believers should be extreme when removing our love for sin,
figuratively (not literally) removing our offensive eye or hand.
The extreme weapon against sin that leads to death is Jesus's
finished work at the cross. May we love Jesus more than sin.

Ichabod

*1 Samuel4:21} And she named the child I-chabod,
saying, The glory is departed from Israel: because the
ark of God was taken, and because of her father in law
and her husband.*

WHEN EXPERIENCING AFFLICTION, THE ONLY WAY TO LIVE
to the glory of God is done in the power of the Holy Spirit.
The risk of falling down a slippery slope into a depression
becomes very real.

Ichabod had to decide if he was to live his life to the glory
of God or fall into a depression. The events surrounding
Ichabod's birth were dire. God's glory was far from the lives
of Ichabod's mother, father, and grandfather, as they all tragi-
cally died as he experienced his first taste of life.

Ichabod's father, Phinehas, was a priest in Israel, as was
Phinehas's father, Eli. Ichabod's father did evil in the sight of
the Lord and his father, Eli did not discipline him well. The
ark of the covenant was Israel's most coveted asset because
the glory of the Lord would dwell with Israel if Israel possessed it. Israel's sinful patterns angered the Lord, and they
lost the ark in battle.

Ichabod's name means loss of glory. Ichabod's mother
felt the affliction of the absence of God's glory with so much
suffering that her body responded with a fatal lament.

Jesus suffered tremendous sadness when rejected and
brutally murdered by those he loved. Ask Jesus for help
when depression sets in so you may live. Jesus was victorious so you can be too.

The Ten Commandments

Galatians {5:22} But the fruit of the Spirit is love, joy,
peace, longsuffering, gentleness, goodness, faith, {5:23}
Meekness, temperance: against such there is no law.

GOD DESIRES HIS PEOPLE TO HAVE A LIFE THAT IS FULL OF
spiritual fruit. Abraham's tiny family grew and enjoyed blessings in Egypt until they became oppressed. God sent Moses
to free the Israelites and show them how to have a righteous
standing before holy God by the law.

The Israelites were accountable for hundreds of laws;
however, God started them off with the ten commandments.
God's people were to serve God alone, no idols of any kind
would be accepted, God's name could never be misused, the
Sabbath would always be considered a holy day, parents were
to be honored; murder, adultery, stealing, lying, and coveting
were never permitted.

Since it is impossible for sinners to perfectly obey the law,
God made a way for the priests to make atonement for them
by ceremonies and sacrificing unblemished animals for the
sins of the people. Since the blood of animals could not fully
atone for sin, God the Father sent the Son to sacrifice precious
blood for the sins of the people.

Sinners love the good news of the gospel. It is good news
that Jesus perfectly obeyed the ten commandments and all
the law, so that we are not judged by them. By the power of
the Holy Spirit, the faithful can repent of their sin and stand
in the righteousness of Jesus by faith. Do you experience
blessed spiritual fruit that only God can provide?

The Guard

Matthew {28:6} He is not here: for he is risen, as he said. Come, see the place where the Lord lay.

DECISIONS ARE OFTEN MADE WITH EMOTIONS WHEN INDIviduals are blinded to the truth. When people lack knowledge or do not want truth, they believe and promote the unthinkable when persuaded.

After the crucifixion of Jesus, the chief priests and the Pharisees requested that Pilate secure the tomb, so to prevent any tampering with the grave. The Jews remembered that Jesus said that the body would not remain in the grave. To protect the Jewish traditions, the tomb had to be secured.

The soldiers standing guard when the angel of the Lord rolled away the stone to Jesus's tomb trembled with the emotion of fear and became like dead men. The watchguards were fearful of the supernatural experience of Jesus's resurrection, as well as fearful of being in breach of contract with their authority.

When the guard reported the events, they were told to spread a lie that Jesus's followers stole the body of Jesus. The emotions of the guard, and their blindness to the truth, allowed them to promote a false story that is perpetuated to this day.

The watchguard over the tomb of the Savoir, like the deceiver, spread a falsehood about Jesus. This enemy of our Lord proudly seeks to lie to those who are blinded to the truth. The truth is that our all-sufficient Savior ended the antagonist's death narrative. Jesus's holy body was not stolen, he is risen!

Judas, Called Barsabbas

*Romans {3:28} Therefore we conclude that a man is
justified by faith without the deeds of the law.*

JUDGING OURSELVES AND OTHERS IN COMPARISON TO THE
standard of perfection leads to the deflated notion that nobody
is good enough. More is the cry of the judge, more obedience,
more sacrifice, and more perfection. Believers can be guilty
of expecting themselves and others to measure up.

As the gospel was being declared to the Gentiles, many
of the Jewish converts began imposing Jewish tradition upon
them. Circumcision was a practice for the Jew but not for the
Gentile. The Jews were pressuring Gentiles to be circumcised
to be declared righteous enough for God.

In Acts 15, Judas called Barsabbas is recorded as involved
with this serious situation. To honor Jesus's mission of grow-
ing the kingdom, many lessons had to be learned. The Jews
were directing the Gentiles to be circumcised to be saved;
however, this was not based on God's plan of redemption
for the Gentiles. In a consensus by the elders and apostles, a
letter was sent to the Gentile believers who needed guidance.
Judas, called Barsabbas, was among the men who served the
Lord and went to the Gentiles in person.

Although the converts were directed to refrain from par-
ticipating in dishonorable pagan practices, they learned that
there was no need to do more. The work of circumcision to
be justified before God was not necessary because salvation
comes by faith in Jesus alone, in accordance with the scriptures, to God's glory.

Goshen

Genesis {46:28} And he sent Judah before him unto Joseph, to direct his face unto Goshen; and they came into the land of Goshen.

BEFORE THE ISRAELITES SUCCUMB TO SLAVERY TO THE Egyptians as a nation of millions, they journeyed from Canaan to Goshen, at Egypt's border, as a family of seventy people. Abraham's descendants were almost extinct from starvation; however, God kept his Messianic promise.

Jacob grieved his son Joseph because Joseph's brothers lied with a tale of his death. When Jacob was an old man, he saw his son Joseph alive as ruler over all the grain in Egypt. There was a famine in the land and Joseph discovered that his family needed help. Joseph invited his family to move to the land of Goshen, a land void of Egyptian affect, yet safe under Egyptian rule.

Joseph safeguarded his family in a prosperous land just far enough from sinful influence by labeling them as shepherds. Shepherds were regarded as beneath Egyptians, and they could not associate. Goshen offered security; however, eventually, Egyptian influence would damage the Israelites. In Goshen, Israel grew from a tiny family to a nation of millions.

Like Goshen was a safeguard for Israel, Jesus is a safeguard for us. Our world may seem safe at first; however, it is not safe. The influence of the world can render us slaves to sin if we are not careful. May we be wise like the enemy and harmless to ourselves and others, safe in Jesus.

The Chief Butler

Genesis {41:9} Then spake the chief butler unto Pharaoh, saying, I do remember my faults this day:

WHEN PAST RECOLLECTIONS ARE TRAUMATIC, THE TENdency is to make every effort to punish or forget the crisis; however, sometimes this is not good. Sometimes, sad things happen for a reason.

The chief butler was an offense, so his master, the Pharaoh, put him in prison. Both the chief butler and the chief baker had disturbing dreams. Joseph, Jacob's eleventh son, was in prison in Egypt, so he interpreted the dreams with good news for the chief butler and sad news for the chief baker. The chief butler was charged to remember Joseph.

The chief butler forgot Joseph for two years, until Pharaoh had disturbing dreams that no one could interpret. The chief butler was returned to his trusted position to Pharaoh, and he did remember Joseph. The chief butler made the best of his dire situation to attain favor and peace of mind for Pharaoh.

Joseph interpreted Pharaoh's dreams by God's will. God revealed, in two separate dreams given to Pharaoh, that there would be seven years of plenty followed by seven years of famine. God used Joseph to save Israel from starvation and from extinction.

Jesus could have punished to death and forgotten sinful humanity for their crisis of rebellion—from Adam in the garden of Eden to the unrepentant men who murdered Jesus— but he did not. The chief butler remembered his promise to Joseph, and Jesus remembered his promise to go to the cross.

Salome

Matthew {20:28} Even as the Son of man came not to be ministered unto, but to minister, and to give his life a ransom for many.

MOTHERS CHARACTERISTICALLY WANT THE BEST FOR their children. Mothers will go to great lengths to encourage, promote, and defend their children because of their love for them. Salome was the mother of the disciples James and John. Salome believed that her sons were to have a special place as judges in God's coming kingdom. Salome made a bold request on behalf of her sons.

Salome recognized a possible eternal advantage to be had for her sons due to their earthly relationship with Jesus, so she requested that her sons be seated on the right and left side of Jesus when he enters his kingdom. Jesus replied that this was a decision for God the Father to make.

Jesus made it clear that unless Salome's sons were able to submit to God's will, as Jesus would submit, then they should not ask for such a gift. Little did Salome know that the will that her sons would share with Jesus would result in their imprisonment and martyrdom.

Salome and her sons learned that the way of Jesus is sacrificial. During the Passover feast, when Jesus knew that the hour had come to leave the world and return to the Father, Jesus washed the feet of his disciples. Washing people's feet was below the task of a Jewish slave. Yet, Jesus, out of love for the disciples set the example of how to serve.

Chapter 11

Luke {4:18}
The Spirit of the Lord
is upon me, because he hath
anointed me to preach the gospel to the poor;
he hath sent me to heal the brokenhearted,
to preach deliverance to the captives, and
recovering of sight to the blind,
to set at liberty them that are bruised,
{4:19} To preach the acceptable year of the Lord.

Bernice

*Acts {26:30} And when he had thus spoken, the king
rose up, and the governor, and Bernice, and they that
sat with them: {26:31} And when they were gone aside,
they talked between themselves, saying, This man doeth
nothing worthy of death or of bonds.*

THE APOSTLE PAUL BOLDLY DECLARED THAT THE DAY OF
the Lord has come and is coming. Paul went from place-to-
place preaching to the Jews and to the Gentiles. The gospel
was intended for the hearer to turn to God in faith, for forgiveness of sins, and eternal life in the name of Jesus.

Bernice was privy to the Jewish mistreatment of Paul.
The Pharisees and the Sadducees disagreed concerning the
hope of the resurrection, this led some Jews to attack Paul.
Roman soldiers arrested Paul and brought him to Governor
Felix. Formal charges could not be found that merited Paul's
imprisonment and possible death sentence, so a hearing took
place in front of Bernice and her husband, King Agrippa.

Bernice wanted to be there to listen as Paul made his
defense to the king. Paul described his conversion from a
Roman Jew who opposed Jesus, to seeing the risen Jesus
and believing.

Scripture teaches that God's Word is never returned void.
It is not clear if Bernice was a curious listener to the hype
of Jesus, or if she became a believer. Today is the perfect
day to tell someone about Jesus. When was the last time
you shared the gospel? Faith only can come by hearing and
receiving God's Word.

Timothy

*Ecclesiastes {10:1} Dead flies cause the ointment
of the apothecary to send forth a stinking savour:
[so doth] a little folly him that is in reputation for
wisdom [and] honour.*

IT IS SURPRISING SOMETIMES HOW THE MOST STEADFAST people can do something so out of character resulting in a discredit to their entire being. Individuals can lose reputations by one bad decision.

In Paul's letter to Timothy, Paul reminds him to fight the good fight of faith. Paul reminds Timothy of his upbringing in the scripture and to never entertain false teaching. Paul encouraged Timothy to lead his congregation well by avoiding controversy and quarrels, to be content, and to be mindful of temptation so to not sin and suffer ruin and destruction.

A young man of good standing, educated in the scriptures from his youth, Timothy had an excellent reputation. Even though Timothy was one who was unlikely to fall into temptation, Paul knew that the devil is seeking to destroy believers. Jesus experienced this when the devil tried to thwart God's redemptive plan by tempting Jesus to disobey and lose credibility as Savior.

Paul knew that every single human can be tempted with the lust of the flesh, the lust of the eyes, and the pride of life, and the only one who could resist sin is Jesus. Once someone loses respect for another they will not want to listen to anything they say. Do not let sin ruin your testimony and alter your life.

Jehiel the Gershonite

*1 Chronicles {29:8} And they with whom [precious]
stones were found gave [them] to the treasure of the
house of the LORD, by the hand of Jehiel the Gershonite.*

IT IS EASY TO GIVE TO THE LORD OUT OF ABUNDANCE, BUT
it is much harder to generously give when there is little. Many
people have shared experiences where they struggled with
giving, only to give and experience God's generous blessings.
I too have had such an experience.

Jehiel the Gershonite beheld a cheerful body of believers
sacrificially giving. King David was nearing the end of his life
and his son Solomon was to fulfill his role as king of Israel
and build God's holy temple in Jerusalem. God's people were
so moved with love for the Lord and inspired by King David's
generosity that they poured out gifts to God.

Jehiel the Gershonite witnessed the evidence of God's generosity. Jesus also witnesses the evidence of God's generosity
of the faithful as they meet the needs of ministry under the
prompting and guidance of the Holy Spirit. God is so generous to supply Jesus to humanity.

On a personal note: I will confess, my husband and I saw
a blessing from giving. Our daughter was to be married and
we wished for an exquisite wedding for Holly. The funds were
saved in full four months prior to the wedding on the condition that we withheld one tithe. After prayer, we cheerfully
gave. After we gave, God miraculously provided the gala and
with funds to spare.

Shimei

2 Samuel {16:5} And when king David came to Bahurim, behold, thence came out a man of the family of the house of Saul, whose name [was] Shimei, the son of Gera: he came forth, and cursed still as he came.

CONFLICT IS AN INESCAPABLE PART OF LIFE. OFTEN PEOPLE are at odds with each other or even within their own conscience because of sin. When confronted by a spirit of judgment, people must know their convictions and be prepared with a strategy to protect their spirit from the attack.

Shimei believed that King David was responsible for the murder of King Saul, so he cursed at David and threw stones. David refused to stop Shimei from the assault, trusting God's will.

Personal sin opens the door for conflict and every repentant heart faces the enemy who comes forth in a rage to curse, harass, and condemn. This harassment can be so terrible that a person may even begin to believe that they are not worthy to be called Christians and miss out on the benefits of Jesus. Jesus offers a strategy for the repentant heart who confesses personal sin.

Shimei accused David like Satan accuses us. Scripture says that there is no condemnation in those who belong to Jesus. May our sin strategy help us to beware of sin because it creates feelings of unworthiness of God's mercy. The curse of sin does not settle on those whose heart is tender toward God, whose hope rests on Jesus's righteousness.

Andrew

*John {1:40} One of the two which heard John [speak,]
and followed him, was Andrew, Simon Peter's brother.
{1:41} He first findeth his own brother Simon, and saith
unto him, We have found the Messias, which is, being
interpreted, the Christ.*

INDIVIDUALS ARE OFTEN LOOKING FOR SOMETHING
better. When something better is identified, it is helpful
to proceed by learning exactly what makes it better from
inspirational people you trust. Once a better thing is realized, it is helpful to then be an inspiration and help others
identify better things too.

Andrew was a fisherman convinced in the promise of the
coming Messiah, and he was inspired by John the Baptist.
Andrew was eagerly looking for the Messiah and he believed
that John was a prophet sent from God to pave the way for
the Messiah. John was an inspiration to Andrew.

John inspired Andrew to regard Jesus as even better, so
Andrew inspired his own brother Simon to learn from Jesus
too. Andrew was among those who demonstrated a heart for
leading people to Christ. Jesus inspired Andrew to respond
to a better profession of being a "fisher of men."

Andrew inspires hearts for missions because he was
among the first to identify that Jesus is better and told
others. Following Jesus is better than following the world
because grace is better than law, mercy is better than punishment, and the gospel is true. Who do you inspire? Who
inspires you? How do you inspire others to know that following Jesus is better?

Sennacherib

2 Chronicles {32:22} Thus the LORD saved Hezekiah and the inhabitants of Jerusalem from the hand of Sennacherib the king of Assyria, and from the hand of all [other,] and guided them on every side.

WHEN THREATENED WITH IMMINENT DANGER, THE HUMAN body's natural response is to either stand firm and fight or run to safety in a flight. This physical response to terror is so common that many people can describe a time when they too made the choice between fight or flight.

Sennacherib was the arrogant king of Assyria who captured God's rebellious people in northern Israel. The people of Judah were Sennacherib's next conquest and he wanted Jerusalem. To terrorize God's faithful people, who prayed and stood firm in their faith, Sennacherib defiantly insulted God. Sennacherib enjoyed threatening Judah's demise.

God's people prayed that the Lord would fight the battle for them, and they trusted that they neither had to fight or flight. Sennacherib lost the battle, and he lost his own life upon his return home. Christians experience threats from the enemy and find comfort, trusting in God's care.

Sennacherib's threats are like the threats many believers face today. As the day draws nearer for Jesus's return, the battle for our trust will grow increasingly difficult. The enemy knows that his time is limited, so he will try to make every day a little harder than the last, as he threatens to capture God's people. Thankfully, Jesus overcomes threatening enemies with power and prayer.

Abner

2 Samuel {3:32} And they buried Abner in Hebron: and the king lifted up his voice, and wept at the grave of Abner; and all the people wept.

LIFE IS BRIEF AND PRECIOUS, AND A GOOD LEGACY IS HARD to leave behind.

Abner was the nephew to King Saul and served his uncle faithfully as commander of Saul's army. Upon King Saul's death, Abner was faithful to his uncle by establishing Saul's son, Ish-bosheth to the throne and by protecting his reign. Ish-bosheth returned the favor by insulting his cousin with an insidious accusation, so Abner defected.

Abner then willed to bring the entire territory of Israel to be joined to Judah under the reign of King David. David's man Joab had his own plan for Abner because Abner murdered Joab's brother during battle, so he murdered Abner in cold blood.

David distanced himself from the crime by giving Abner a proper funeral, and his is the most detailed funeral recorded in the Old Testament. King David gave Abner a respectable funeral and honored Abner as a man with a good legacy, although Abner did not deserve it.

Abner reminds how Jesus wants to give his faithful a good legacy, even though none can end well on their own. Sinners are born with a tarnished legacy and do not deserve to end well because of the sin that separates people from God forever. Jesus came from heaven to reconcile sinners to God by granting the faithful a new legacy in righteousness, so we may end well.

Euodias

Philippians {4:2} I beseech Euodias, and beseech Syn-
tyche, that they be of the same mind in the Lord.

THE BIGGEST HINDRANCE TO CHRISTIAN GROWTH IS SIN.
When sin is left unchecked, it will destroy our testimony for
the Lord. Sin gets in the way of ministry.

Euodias was a minister of the gospel of Jesus and was
having such a terrible disagreement with another woman
in ministry that the news reached Paul while in prison. In
Paul's letter to the Philippians, he encourages the church of
Philippi to be mature in eternal matters, to stand firm in the
faith, and to agree in the Lord.

It is natural to have a disagreement with someone, to
become offended by their words, or be tempted to have an
open argument. Euodias would have done well to listen to
Paul and follow the example of fellow believers, who are filled
with the Holy Spirit when in a difficult relational experience.
When we have an all-out dispute with a fellow believer, we
pridefully reject Jesus.

Jesus would have us go to the person who is offended and
work it out right away. If the first private meeting does not
bring peace, then scripture says to try again and bring another
believer. Do not let time go by before trying to reconcile a
relationship with a fellow believer. This allows for confused
details and fosters hatred to grow. Forsake those who are
unwilling to work out differences because they are rebellious
against God. Christians are called to love each other.

Abishai

2 Samuel {16:9} Then said Abishai the son of Zeruiah unto the king, Why should this dead dog curse my lord the king? Let me go over, I pray thee, and take off his head.

IT IS NATURAL TO REACT IN A HOSTILE MANNER WHEN being criticized unjustly. Rarely will it be helpful to reciprocate hostility for hostility because of the risk of escalated violence. Handling criticism with a positive attitude is an attribute that takes thought and practice. Seeking God's guidance to willingly do his will when facing a hostile person takes wisdom.

King David faced the hostile Shimei who cursed him and threw rocks. Abishai, one of King David's mighty men, was ready to take action to stop the insults thrown at his king.

Abishai offered to avenge King David with the murder of Shimei; however, David had the wisdom to trust the Lord and to let God's will be done. David did not believe that Abishai had the correct advice that would bring God glory. God will defend honor.

Abishai offered bad advice; however, Jesus offers the best advice by the power of the Holy Spirit. God imparts wisdom on his faithful followers when they spend time in prayer and reading the Bible. People are often willing to offer advice, so consider the source. Advice like that of Abishai was not good and King David was wise to reject it. Ask Jesus for wisdom when handling criticism and hostility, he is faithful and promises that you will receive it.

Hiram, King of Tyre

1 Kings {5:1} And Hiram king of Tyre sent his servants unto Solomon; for he had heard that they had anointed him king in the room of his father: for Hiram was ever a lover of David.

TIMES OF PEACE COME WHEN WISE LEADERS GOVERN LAW-abiding people. When a leader oversees a nation walking obediently in laws that govern fair and well, then there is a pathway for peace.

King Solomon enjoyed peace through his vast kingdom. Times of peace are honorable to the Lord, and during times of peace it is fitting to honor God abundantly. Hiram, king of Tyre, was a Gentile who esteemed God and honored God's people. Hiram loved King David and loved King Solomon. When the time came time for King Solomon to build God's temple, God used Hiram.

Hiram provided the perfect material, cedar from Lebanon, so to provide a suitable dwelling place for God to dwell with his people. Little did Hiram know that one day, God's people would exchange their peace with God in the beautiful temple for a life of sin and ruin.

Jesus provided the perfect material, righteousness from eternity, so to provide a suitable dwelling place in the regenerated hearts of humanity. Jesus knew that God's people would reject him, still he gave his own life, death, and resurrection for all who will love him.

We live among unpeaceful people who favor laws lacking in wisdom. People fall victim to ruin because of sin; however, a time of peace is coming because Jesus obediently went to the cross.

Jairus

Mark {5:35} While he yet spake, there came from the ruler
of the synagogue's [house certain] which said, Thy daughter
is dead: why troublest thou the Master any further?

WHEN A PERSON IS EXPERIENCING PHYSICAL OR EMO-
tional danger, the first emotive instinct is usually fear. These
days, fear grips us all every now and again.

Jairus was a ruler in the synagogue, a loyal Jew, who
believed Jesus was a healer sent from God. Jairus made his
way through the crowd of people to fall on Jesus's feet, begging Jesus to come to his home to heal his dying daughter.

As Jesus and Jairus walked, Jesus was delayed by a faithful woman with a bloody issue who touched the hem of his
garment and was healed. Jesus cared for the woman as Jairus
was fearful for his daughter. Jairus's fears were overcome by
his belief when Jesus told him to believe and not to fear. Jesus
brought Jairus's daughter back from the dead.

Whether you are fearful in a life-and-death situation like
Jairus was, fearful for basic provisions, or fearful of God's judgment of sin, remember a spirit of fearfulness is not from God.

The Holy Spirit dwells in the hearts of believers so to
comfort the fearful. The Father provides for the little birds
and the lilies of the field, and believers can trust that God will
provide much more for those who love Jesus. God's perfect
love drives out fear and replaces it with a peace that passes
all understanding. Jesus delivers us from fear.

Lazarus

John {11:35} Jesus wept.

THE PASSING OF A CHERISHED PERSON IS BY FAR ONE OF the utmost losses anyone can encounter. The finality of losing the opportunity to create new memories with a loved one on this side of heaven is gripping. The realization that the memories of the deceased cease to be communicated on this side of heaven is also devastating.

To demonstrate that Jesus was truly a human man and truly God in the flesh at the same time, he would perform miracles that no regular man could accomplish. Jesus would heal people from their blindness and from infirmities, he would cast demons out of people, feed thousands of people with small quantities of food, walk on water, and more.

Jesus loved Lazarus and Lazarus's sisters, Mary and Martha. Jesus was mistreated by the Jewish leaders and was staying outside of Jerusalem when he learned that Lazarus was sick to the point of death. Jesus purposefully waited two days before setting out on the long and risky journey to Bethany. Upon arrival, Jesus was moved to sorrow as he and his friends grieved Lazarus.

Jesus resurrected Lazarus, and after this, many people believed that Jesus was the Son of God. From that point on, the Jewish leaders began to plan the death of Jesus to preserve their nation and continue their priestly roles in the temple. Jesus wept because death is painful. Death resulting from sin is final; however, death to sin by the work of Jesus is the hope of eternal life.

The Man Who Was Possessed

*Mark {5:18} And when he was come into the ship,
he that had been possessed with the devil prayed him
that he might be with him.*

THE MAN WHO WAS POSSESSED WAS BEYOND HELPING, EVEN the strongest chains could not stop his self-mutilation. This tortured man had only one hope, Jesus, who healed him.

The man who was possessed loved Jesus for saving him from a hopeless, horrible life. The man wished to follow Jesus; however, he honored Jesus's wish for him to go and tell everyone all about the miraculous healing he received. When fully understood, the law, gospel, grace, and mercy all merit generous boasting to our friends, family, and any who will listen.

In Luke, Jesus uses a parable to make an example of a woman who sought to honor him generously with the anointing of expensive oil. Jesus revealed how people with large sin debts to forgive will feel more thankful to Jesus than people with little sin debts to forgive. Jesus points out that the woman with oil had committed many sins, so she is more loving and generous toward Jesus. In contrast, people who do not recognize the cancellation of their sin debt as something extra valuable will love Jesus less.

May believers in Jesus never undervalue Christ's work on the cross. May believers marvel at the loving grace of God, who mercifully planned from eternity to condescend from glory, die, and conquer the grave for sinners. Are you quick to tell everyone about your love for Jesus?

Matthew

Matthew {9:9} And as Jesus passed forth from thence,
he saw a man, named Matthew, sitting at the receipt
of custom: and he saith unto him, Follow me. And he
arose, and followed him.

THERE ARE SOME "RAGS TO RICHES" STORIES THAT CANNOT be denied because they inspire hope. Not many popular story lines feature characters who trade in their riches for rags.

Jewish tax collectors who collected the tax for Rome were not favored by their peers. Many tax collectors were extortionists. Matthew was a tax collector for Rome, so naturally his was not a good name to have.

Matthew was content with his comfortable role; however, the effectual call by Jesus's grace was irresistible. Matthew left his social status with the wealthy in exchange for a position with poor, lost, and sinful humans.

At first, Matthew's story seemed to be one from riches to rags; however, his story is a "rags to riches" tale. Matthew's reward was greater than all he gave up because Matthew taught sinners about Christ and salvation to further grow the kingdom of God. Matthew traded sin for eternal life and God's glory.

Jesus too gave up riches when he left heaven to become a man and identify with ragged humanity. The perfect Son of God put on sin so to bring many sons to glory. Jesus now sits on the throne in the heavenly places seeking to bless Christians with the riches of eternal life and glory in exchange for the rags of death.

Chapter 12

Exodus {33:18}
And he said,
I beseech thee,
shew me thy glory.

Noadiah

Nehemiah {6:14} My God, think thou upon Tobiah and Sanballat according to these their works, and on the prophetess Noadiah, and the rest of the prophets, that would have put me in fear.

THERE IS AN ELEMENT OF SADNESS IN LIFE WHEN WE DIScover our enemies. Satan is constantly roaming and seeking to deter followers of Jesus. Trusted people in our lives can be Satan's instruments. The stronger our relationship is with God, the more we recognize our enemies.

God used Babylon to punish the Jews with the destruction of the temple, the burning of the city of Jerusalem, and carrying off the Israelites into captivity. Seventy years after the Babylon exile, the Israelites slowly began to return to their promised land. After the temple restoration in Jerusalem, God used Nehemiah to lead the Israelites in the rebuilding of the walls that surrounded and protected the city.

Noadiah was a prophetess who aided God's enemies in trying to scare and deter the Jews from their work in Jerusalem. Noadiah and her peers prophesied that Nehemiah must hide or be killed. Nehemiah was not deterred by Noadiah because God helped him.

Jesus's enemy tried to deter Jesus from doing God's will, so to receive glory on earth and bypass the cross. Jesus was not deterred from holy living and dying for humanity. Do not be sad when you recognize your enemies because God is in control. Jesus holds us tight in his strength, so we are not deterred. *Matthew {5:44} But I say unto you, Love your enemies, bless them that curse you, do good to them that hate you, and pray for them.*

Bartimaeus

Mark {10:46} And they came to Jericho: and as he went out of Jericho with his disciples and a great number of people, blind Bartimaeus, the son of Timaeus, sat by the highway side begging.

FAITH IS NOT SOMETHING SOMEONE CAN CHOOSE TO obtain; it cannot be put on; faith must be put in by God. Faith is a miraculous belief without doubtless proof.

Many people are walking around in a condition called spiritual blindness, and it causes people to doubt God. Spiritual blindness is cured when God simultaneously opens the hearts of believers to receive the gift of faith, while believers are hearing the gospel message and requesting forgiveness of sin and eternal life in Jesus's name.

Bartimaeus was a blind man in his physical body but not in his spirit. Bartimaeus recognized Jesus as the promised Messiah. Bartimaeus trusted the King of Heaven, who came from the lineage of the family of David, to make him well.

Bartimaeus cried out to Jesus for healing so loud that many tried to quiet him. Bartimaeus trusted in Jesus with loud pleas to have his sight restored, he trusted wholeheartedly that his request would be granted out of God's mercy. Bartimaeus's faith in Jesus made him well, faith freely given by grace, not works.

Believers now look back to the cross and see what Jesus did for humanity with humble adoration. Believers look forward to the kingdom of heaven with great hope and anticipation because of what Jesus has prepared. Spiritual blindness is overcome by Jesus's marvelous light.

The Woman at En-rogel

2 Samuel {17:19} And the woman took and spread a covering over the well's mouth, and spread ground corn thereon; and the thing was not known.

WHEN THE FAITHFUL RECOGNIZE GOD'S SOVEREIGNTY, they begin to act according to God's will, even if it means risking one's own security.

The woman at En-rogel knew that the kingdom of Israel was being threatened. King David's power-hungry son, Absalom, gathered his army to defeat the army of David, to kill his father, and to claim the throne. David was awaiting word in the wilderness from his allies who were consulting with his enemies undercover. David needed to learn how to defend against Absalom and his men. The message that David needed from his allies was critical for survival.

The woman at En-rogel risked her own security to hide the allies of King David in her well, so enemies could not prevent them from delivering the critical message. Absalom planned to delay the attack on his father, King David. There was time for a counterattack. Absalom was defeated, and David was restored to the throne of Israel.

Jesus protects the faithful by hiding away the sin that leads to death by his own righteousness. At the cross, the sovereign will of God was fulfilled when the Messiah died for humanity and restored their fellowship with God. Humanity may now live forever in God's Spirit, but they need to hear the gospel. May the faithful learn how to share the critical message of the gospel.

Uriah

Psalm {51:1} Have mercy upon me, O God, according to thy lovingkindness: according unto the multitude of thy tender mercies blot out my transgressions. {51:2} Wash me throughly from mine iniquity, and cleanse me from my sin. {51:4} Against thee, thee only, have I sinned, and done [this] evil.

THE OPPOSITE OF HONOR IS SHAME. WHEN INDIVIDUALS are honorable, they have value in their own eyes, in the eyes of their peers, and in the eyes of those who are superior. Protecting one's honor is important to maintain respect and prevent being regarded with shame.

Uriah the Hittite was the husband of a beautiful woman named Bathsheba. King David sent for Bathsheba, and she conceived while Uriah was performing his honorable duty as a top warrior in battle. To cover the indiscretion, David brought Uriah home from the battlefield to be with his wife, to shift the paternity; however, Uriah would not dishonor his men who were at war or the ark of the covenant that was with them. Upon return to battle, King David had Uriah murdered so he could marry the widow, Bathsheba. King David grieved his sin and prayed to be restored to God. Psalm 51 is David's lament.

Uriah was honorable in both life and in death; however, Jesus is most honorable because he did not sin. Repentance was learned by King David because of the honor of Uriah. All sin is dishonor to God, and sin merits repentance. When you sin, repent and be restored to God, he is faithful to forgive.

Jephthah

Matthew {5:37} But let your communication be,
Yea, yea; Nay, nay: for whatsoever is more than these
cometh of evil.

TAKING AN OATH IS A CUSTOMARY PRACTICE IN MOST places in the world. A marriage vow, an oath of citizenship, a fiduciary oath, an oath of public office, and an oath to testify in court are all familiar promises that are made to swear that a person's word is true. Oaths should be necessary.

Jephthah was an illegitimate warrior who was forced out of his home when he was an adult. When his brothers realized that they needed his skill in the battlefield, and they saw his great faith in God, they sought to bring him back to make him a leader.

During a battle against the Ammonites, Jephthah made a solemn oath to the Lord. Jephthah promised that he would sacrifice the first thing that he saw upon returning home if the Lord would give him victory. The first thing Jephthah saw upon return was the last thing he wanted to sacrifice. Jephthah's oath came at an ultimate price, the painful separation between himself and his only child. Oaths should be necessary, and people are to keep their word.

Jephthah made an unnecessary oath; however, our Lord made an oath with purpose and God kept the promise. From eternity, God lovingly promised to send his Son to pay the ultimate price for sin, to reconcile humanity in righteousness. Jesus Christ kept the oath to be our Savior.

The Jailer

Acts {16:33} And he took them the same hour of the night, and washed [their] stripes; and was baptized, he and all his, straightway.

WHEN PEOPLE OF FAITH WORSHIP GOD, WHILE IN A CRISIS, they inspire others to want to know more about Jesus. God gives us more than we can manage, so we can be helped in his strength.

The followers of Jesus bravely broke all the rules surrounding preaching in Jesus's name and happily went to jail for it. The jailer knew full well that his life was in danger if he mismanaged the imprisoned Christians, so when an earthquake allowed for the prisoners to escape, the jailer was ready to take his own life for failing at his post.

The prisoners did not escape, and they stopped the jailer from harming himself. As a result, the jailer personally rescued the Christians and was baptized straightaway with his family. The jailer was saved to eternal life because of the witness of his prisoners. Jail is a horrible place, yet the disciples were singing to the Lord, encouraging each other, and filled with peace.

This peace is freely offered to all believers by God through the gift of faith in the Lord Jesus Christ. God has a plan and purpose for each day of our lives. Some days will be better than others. The world is listening to God's faithful and watching their conduct in both good and tough times. Let them hear us proclaim Jesus's goodness, faithfulness, and love on every occasion.

The Firstfruits

Deuteronomy {18:4} The firstfruit [also] of thy corn, of thy wine, and of thine oil, and the first of the fleece of thy sheep, shalt thou give him.

BEING GENEROUS DOES NOT COME EASILY FOR EVERYONE. By being transformed into the likeness of Jesus, who gives grace and mercy generously, the faithful can easily be generous.

God generously revealed to Moses all about how he wanted to bless people. The Levitical priesthood was made up of those from the tribe of Levi whose duty was to make atonement for the sins of God's people. With some exception, the priests would have no provisions, they were to depend on the Lord's firstfruits, the food offerings, as their inheritance for their ministry.

Each year, a festival was celebrated to honor the Lord with the best of the first harvest from the ground. The people were to bring a basket of their first and best harvest to honor God. The firstfruits represented a joyful celebration of the hope for the generous harvest that was to come.

The indwelling Holy Spirit is the believer's firstfruits of the hope of heaven. The kingdom that God has prepared supersedes this present time, and our hope is in that which we do not see.

One sweet day, believers will move beyond the firstfruits to a glorious harvest, where we will be set free from the temptation to sin and from the effects of sin. Sinful bodies that have died will generously be resurrected and glorified with life unimaginable because of Jesus's righteousness.

Isaac

Hebrews {11:20} By faith Isaac blessed Jacob and Esau
concerning things to come.

A RELATIONSHIP THAT IS LACKING TRUST IS A RELATION-
ship in ruin.

The faithful are to accept that testing is a part of life. Trials
and tests from God are helpful to believers to prove their faith
in God to themselves and to those around them. No test will
cause our faith to fail because God promises to not test us
beyond our ability to prevail in God's power.

Isaac was the son of Abraham who received the Messianic
promise. Isaac's descendants would outnumber the stars in
the sky and would yield the Savior of the world, Jesus, to the
nation of Israel. Isaac was the promised son, whom Sarah
bore to Abraham when she was ninety years old.

Trusting God came naturally for Abraham. When God
told Abraham to sacrifice his beloved son, Isaac, on an altar,
he journeyed for three days trusting God. When the time
came to offer Isaac, God withheld him, an angel stopped
Abraham. God provided a substitutionary sacrifice so that
Isaac would live. God did not withhold his only Son, Jesus
Christ, our substitutionary sacrifice.

Isaac trusted God. Upon his deathbed, he was tricked
and unintentionally blessed his second-born twin son, Jacob,
instead of his firstborn, Esau. Isaac trusted God's will and
would not take the Messianic blessing back from Jacob to the
heartbreak of his firstborn son.

Trials and testing occur often. God uses faithful believers
to show the world what it looks like to trust in Jesus.

Demas

Matthew {13:3} And he spake many things unto them in parables, saying, Behold, a sower went forth to sow.

ONE OF THE MOST HEARTBREAKING THINGS THAT CAN happen in the Christian community is seeing a follower of Jesus walk away from their faith.

Demas was a colleague to the Apostle Paul, a fellow worker in the Lord. Paul wrote to Timothy and advised that when he was under attack he was abandoned by Demas because his cares for the world were more important than cares for eternity.

Many individuals who hear and receive the gospel turn away during a time of hardship. Jesus taught a parable referencing a sower of seed, to explain various responses to the gospel.

Jesus explained to the disciples that the seed is the gospel, and the soil is the human heart. When a person does not understand the gospel, the devil takes away the seed that was planted, sown. Some seeds fall on rocky ground and are received with joy for a while, until hardship occurs and they retreat. The person who receives the seed that grows, because of the gift of faith and understanding, belongs to God.

Demas walked away from God because his heart was not with God. Jesus will never walk away from the church and the faithful of God will never walk away from Jesus. God designed the human heart to love Jesus and to walk righteously, in free will. Praise God for a new heart that can genuinely love Jesus.

The Miracles

*Hebrews {2:3} How shall we escape, if we neglect so
great salvation; which at the first began to be spoken
by the Lord, and was confirmed unto us by them that
heard [him;]{2:4} God also bearing [them] witness,
both with signs and wonders, and with divers miracles,
and gifts of the Holy Ghost, according to his own will?*

PEOPLE WHO ARE NEW TO THE MIRACLE OF SALVATION
often wrestle with their responsibility in their newfound
journey to glory. It is tempting to use the law as a standard;
however, obeying the law cannot contribute to the miracle
of salvation. The accuser is always condemning believers for
sin, trying to stop their growth to glory.

God is famous for miracles. Miracles in nature, such as
the virgin birth of Jesus and his walk on water, bear witness
to God's spirituality. Miracles of healing, such as Miriam's
leprosy, bear witness to both God's wrath and mercy. Miracles
of God's will, such as the freeing of his people from slavery in
Egypt, bear witness to God's sovereignty. Miracles of provision, such as water coming from a rock in the desert or closing
the mouths of the lions in Daniel's den, bear witness to God's
omnipresence. Miracles of resurrection, such as Elijah raising
the widow's son or Jesus's resurrection, bear witness to God's
power, love, and glory.

Salvation is nothing short of a miracle and Jesus is
the miracle worker who saves us from sin. Righteousness
before God comes no other way except by Jesus's miraculous work at the cross.

Jonah

*Jonah {3:9} Who can tell [if] God will turn and repent,
and turn away from his fierce anger, that we perish not?*

JONAH WAS FAMILIAR WITH THE GREAT LOVE GOD HAD
for the nation of Israel. Jonah saw how God continued to
bless Israel, even furthering its borders, though the nation
was disobedient under wicked kings.

When God spoke to Jonah and told him to go to Nineveh
and call out against it for its evil ways, Jonah fled. Jonah preferred to run from the presence of the Lord rather than go
to Nineveh. Jonah boarded a boat headed to Tarshish, going
in the opposite direction, to flee from God.

Jonah sailed away, so God sent a storm. Jonah preferred
death over obedience and having a part in saving an unworthy nation. The pagan sailors identified Jonah as the cause
of the raging storm. After praying for forgiveness and going
against their conscience, they hurled Jonah off the boat at
Jonah's request, and the storm ceased. God sent a great fish
to rescue Jonah by swallowing him near the bottom of the
sea. Jonah prayed a prayer of thanksgiving, and God made
the fish vomit Jonah onto the land, so he may go to Nineveh.

God turned his fierce anger away from Nineveh. Jonah's
account in scriptures does not mean that God changed his
mind, rather the message is that God is forgiving to all the
nations, not just Israel. God used Jonah to show mercy to
Nineveh just like Jesus shows mercy to every nation.

Delilah

Judges {16:18} And when Delilah saw that he had told her all his heart, she sent and called for the lords of the Philistines, saying, Come up this once, for he hath shewed me all his heart.

THE PHILISTINES WERE FRUSTRATED WITH DELILAH'S strong man, Samson, because he caused a great deal of damage to them. Samson could not be subdued for his strength was superior to every man around him, as he was a Nazirite from birth.

When the Philistines learned that Delilah was having an affair with Samson, who was a judge in Israel, they offered her a great sum of silver in exchange for the secret to his strength. Day after day, Delilah asked Samson about his secret, and he would tell her lie after lie. Each time Samson told Delilah a lie, she tested it and called in the Philistines to capture him; however, he would overpower them each time. Finally, he gave in and revealed his secret, a razor never touched his hair, once his hair was cut, he was weakened and subdued.

God used Delilah's motive for money to remind that even a Nazirite to God can be linked with foolishness leading to a legacy of death. Upon Samson's death, thousands of Philistines died. Jesus motivates the faithful to help each other live well, to cling to people who love God, and to value eternity, so to do well. God uses Jesus's motive for loving fellowship to remind that God desires a legacy of eternal life in the Holy Spirit.

Darius

Daniel {6:25} Then king Darius wrote unto all people, nations, and languages, that dwell in all the earth; Peace be multiplied unto you. {6:26} I make a decree, That in every dominion of my kingdom men tremble and fear before the God of Daniel: for he is the living God.

THE PROPHET DANIEL EXPLAINED TO BELSHAZZAR, KING of Babylon, the fatal message written by God's finger during his blasphemous revelry. Belshazzar's time was up, he was to be eliminated and a new king, King Darius, was to be made king overnight.

The Spirit of God was with Daniel as he was held captive in Babylon. King Darius valued Daniel and was to establish him over the kingdom. Daniel's enemies knew that to remove Daniel from King Darius's favor they must find a way to reveal Daniel's allegiance to God as above his allegiance to King Darius. Daniel's enemies had King Darius sign a decree, which could not be reversed, so that anyone praying to anything other than King Darius for thirty days would be cast into the lions' den.

This decree did not stop Daniel from facing Jerusalem three times a day to pray, so Daniel was thrown into the lions' den. King Darius was glad when he discovered that God protected Daniel by shutting the mouths of the lions. Daniel's enemies were thrown to those lions and destroyed.

Darius fulfilled the law and threw Daniel to the lions for praying to God. Jesus too fulfilled the law by laying down his own life for the forgiveness of sin, while praying for the enemies.

The Oil

Exodus {30:25} And thou shalt make it an oil of holy ointment, an ointment compound after the art of the apothecary: it shall be an holy anointing oil.

PEOPLE TEND TO SEPARATE SPECIAL THINGS. GOD DESIRES to dwell with a special people and this requires that they be separated from sin. God revealed his holiness to the people by the law and revealed his desire to dwell with people by the covering of sin. To satisfy God's wrath against sin, the innocent had to die for the guilty upon the altar. God used oil to purify the sacrifice and to evidence God's will.

God instructed the priests to burn oil for light and to include oil in the regular grain offering. The holy anointing oil was specially prepared by a perfumer for the purpose of anointing God's people. The prophet Samuel used oil to anoint Saul to be king of Israel, and after that, he anointed King David. Zadok anointed Solomon with oil to reveal God's will for the next king. King Jesus was anointed with a costly, perfumed oil called nard, days before he died.

In the Old Testament, the anointing of oil was an exterior symbol representing the inner working of the Holy Spirit, who changes a person's heart to love God's will. The New Testament sheds light on God's anointing oil by filling believers with the Holy Spirit. The anointing oil of the Spirit sets the faithful apart from the world, for holiness, for good works, and to do God's will.

Chapter 13

———◈✦◈———

Acts {2:42}
And they continued stedfastly
in the apostles'
doctrine and fellowship,
and in breaking of bread,
and in prayers.

Chloe

*1 Corinthians {1:11} For it hath been declared unto me
of you, my brethren, by them [which are of the house]
of Chloe, that there are contentions among you.*

THERE ARE MULTIPLE REASONS FOR A PERSON TO BELONG
to a local church beyond the fact that scripture teaches
believers to gather regularly for worship. Church provides
a place for encouragement, allows the exercise of spiritual
gifts, offers a place to bear one another's burdens and to
praise God for his goodness. Church gives a place for the
honor of the sacraments of baptism and communion, for
reading the Bible aloud, praying, and singing God's praises
that will continue with us into eternity.

Sometimes divisive people will make church uncomfortable by their pettiness in things like dress code, music, bud-
geting, or the like. Divisive people can make church a very
unhappy place, especially when they move beyond the petty
and divide the members on serious faith issues.

Chloe's people were peacemakers who demonstrated a wise
example by bringing Paul a report of dissension within the
church body. The divisive followers were quarreling because
they were more focused on the eloquence of their ministers
rather than the message of Jesus. This allowed for clarification
on the importance of unity and oneness in the Spirit.

Unfortunately, sometimes people create disunity in
church. A person with a divisive spirit can create havoc on a
church family. Divisive people need prayer, love, and unity,
too. Pray for church leadership and members to embrace
those with a contentious spirit with gentleness, for God's glory.

Esau

Genesis {27:38} And Esau said unto his father, Hast thou but one blessing, my father? bless me, [even] me also, O my father. And Esau lifted up his voice, and wept.

THINGS DO NOT ALWAYS GO ACCORDING TO PLAN. GOD works in mysterious ways as he works out his sovereign will for his glory, and we cannot understand his wisdom.

Abraham was known to be a faithful friend to God. Abraham and his son Isaac both believed that God's promised Savior would one day be born through their exclusive lineage. Isaac's firstborn son, Esau, was a man who put his flesh before his faith when he verbally sold his birthright to his twin, Jacob, for a pot of lentils. As the firstborn son, it was Esau's legal right to claim his father's inheritance; however, his mother Rebekah remembered God's answered prayer as to why her twins wrestled in her womb. The older son would serve the younger son.

Rebekah believed that the Messiah would come from the family lineage of Jacob and not Esau. When Isaac was old, he was to bless his firstborn son, Esau. Rebekah conducted a deceptive plan that tricked Isaac into giving the Messianic blessing to Jacob instead of Esau.

When Esau learned that he lost this blessing, he pleaded with his father. Esau begged his father for a blessing that only his father could give. Jesus pleads to God the Father for the blessing of eternal life for believers, a blessing that only the Father can give. Jesus is pleading to the Father for you.

Phinehas, Son of Eleazar

Joshua {22:34} And the children of Reuben and the
children of Gad called the altar [Ed:] for it [shall be] a
witness between us that the LORD [is] God.

A KEEPSAKE LIKE A MONUMENT OR A STATUE CAN REMIND
of something comforting and worthy of acknowledgment
for generations. One such altar was erected by some of the
descendants of Jacob just outside of the promised land boundaries. The tribes created this monument to serve as a witness
to the generations to come that their identity was with the
nation of Israel. The altar was not well received by the other
tribes because there was to be only one altar for God.

The nation of Israel did not want to be punished for the
sins of these tribes, so it sent Phinehas—along with ten chiefs,
one from each of the tribal families of Israel, everyone being
the head of their clan—to inquire. Phinehas approached
the rebellious tribes regarding the offensive, imposing altar.
Phinehas learned that the tribes wanted to be sure that they
would never lose their identity apart from Israel. Phinehas
understood the fear that the generations to come could forget
that they were God's chosen nation.

Phinehas found honor in the keepsake memento that
allowed the tribes to identify with Israel as belonging to God,
so no war was necessary. Jesus's followers keep the visible
keepsakes of the ordinances of baptism and the communion
of the Lord's Supper, so to identify with the risen Savior and
look forward to his return. Keepsakes are comforting.

The Red Sea

Hebrews {11:29} By faith they passed through the Red sea as by dry [land:] which the Egyptians assaying to do were drowned.

IN A WORLD FULL OF THEOLOGIANS, IT CAN BE DIFFICULT to differentiate the truth from the almost truth. With so many Christian denominations, religious organizations, and televangelists to choose from, some will simply settle for the faith path of least resistance.

God did not let Israel choose the path of least resistance. When the time came for God to keep the promise to rescue Abraham's descendants from their four-hundred-year bondage in Egypt, God sent Moses to lead. The Israelites found themselves trapped between Egyptian soldiers and the Red Sea.

Moses obeyed God and parted the waters so that Israel could walk safely to the other side. As the Egyptian soldiers followed, God caused the waters to fill again, and the Egyptian soldiers died. God fought for his people in a manner that allowed them to press on toward victory against all odds, fighting the good fight of faith.

The world is full of people who are trapped between sin and death, like the Egyptians who perished in the Red Sea. Many different faiths try to lead to God but do not embrace the hard truths about following Jesus. The path of least resistance easily misleads. Jesus parted the waters of sin and death by the cross and believers face resistance to the gospel. Jesus fought and won the victory over sin and death, so all may pass through to eternal life by faith.

Stephen

Acts {7:59} And they stoned Stephen, calling upon
[God,] and saying, Lord Jesus, receive my spirit.

IT TAKES A GREAT DEAL OF FAITH TO ASK GOD FOR WISDOM.
The one who gains wisdom also searches for understanding,
so to demonstrate them in both word and deed. Having the
discernment to acquire God's wisdom and understanding
requires the work of the Holy Spirit.

It is written of Stephen that he was a man of great faith,
full of the Holy Spirit. Stephen welcomed the appointment
to help distribute food to the widows of the early church. In
addition to Stephen's modest labor, it is recorded that Stephen
risked his life to rebuke the Jews who rejected Jesus.

In Stephen's wisdom, he expounded the scriptures beginning with Abraham to a crowd of defiant Jews who were
clinging to their old ways of practicing the laws of Moses unto
their righteousness. The more Stephen spoke in the power of
the Spirit the more defiant the crowd became. Stephen was
not afraid to boldly share his wisdom of the scripture, nor
was he afraid to stand up to the wickedness of his fellow Jews.

Nothing worth anything comes easy and faith is worth
pursuing. For many people around the world, this gift
of faith comes at the cost of death. Stephen was the first
recorded martyr for Christ; however, he was not the last.
Every day, wise Christians who are full of understanding
follow Stephen's lead, to shun the wicked and share the
gospel, risking their death.

The Canaanite Woman

Matthew {15:27} And she said, Truth, Lord: yet the dogs eat of the crumbs which fall from their masters' table.

GOD CHOSE THE NATION OF ISRAEL TO BE A BLESSING TO all the nations of the world; however, Israel was to be first to receive the miraculous gifts of signs and wonders from the Messiah. The Jews were watching and waiting for their Savior to come through the house of David, yet they did not recognize Jesus as their king. A Canaanite woman, with some knowledge of the Jewish law, did recognize Jesus as the Messiah. She learned that Jesus was working miracles, so she went to him.

The Canaanite woman begged Jesus to heal her daughter. Jesus refused the gentile woman because his blessing was not for her, but for the lost sheep of Israel. Jesus tested her faith, referring to her as a domesticated little dog, who should not get bread designated for the children. The woman's faith was strong, begging Jesus to remember that even the pups rejoice in the crumbs that fall from the table. Jesus's power to heal the Canaanite woman's daughter related to the condition of her heart. The woman cried out in faith and Jesus loved her, he miraculously healed her daughter in that moment.

When crying out to God, remember that Jesus hears you and acts with wisdom and sovereignty. God's perfect order, planning, direction, and consistency are trustworthy. God is always good, so we may be confident to cry out to God with faith because he loves us.

Jesse

1 Samuel {16:1} And the LORD said unto Samuel, How long wilt thou mourn for Saul, seeing I have rejected him from reigning over Israel? fill thine horn with oil, and go, I will send thee to Jesse the Bethlehemite: for I have provided me a king among his sons.

GOD'S CHOSEN PEOPLE—FROM ABRAHAM, ISAAC, JACOB, Judah, Boaz, and descendants to Jesse—were all looking with hope to the coming of the Messiah. They had eager anticipation for the man God would send to become king of Israel, to redeem and rule God's people forever.

God gave Israel its first king, who was Saul; however, God rejected Saul and sought to have the prophet Samuel anoint the next king, the king who would be a man after God's own heart. Jesse, the grandson of Boaz from Bethlehem, was invited to welcome the prophet Samuel to a sacrifice in his home, where the Lord would choose one of his sons to be anointed. Jesse likely did not know the importance of the occasion because not all of his sons were invited.

God rejected all of Jesse's sons, leaving Samuel wondering why, so he asked Jesse if there were any sons missing. Jesse's son David was tending the sheep. Samuel anointed David with oil, according to God's command, in the presence of his brothers. David was then filled with the Holy Spirit. Jesse's hope for the Messiah was increased in his youngest son, David. Jesse's descendant, the eternal king, is the Lord Jesus Christ.

The Unauthorized Fire

Leviticus {10:1} And Nadab and Abihu, the sons of Aaron, took either of them his censer, and put fire therein, and put incense thereon, and offered strange fire before the LORD, which he commanded them not.

HAVING A RIGHT VIEW OF GOD WILL TRANSFORM A PERSON from being repugnant in the eyes of the Lord. Sin is unacceptable to holy God. As God's priests learned about holiness and sin, bad choices were made.

Moses's brother Aaron was the first from the tribe of Levi to be a priest to God. Priests brought God and people together in righteousness. Nadab and Abihu, Aaron's sons, were learning the priesthood; however, they were found to be repugnant by doing that which was forbidden, and they died. Exodus chapter 30:9 forbids unauthorized fire, incense, or offerings before the Lord.

Looking around, it is not hard to see that many believers are trapped in unauthorized worship practices that take glory away from Jesus. Shifting glory, praise, and worship to humankind is done in subtle ways that are often hard to identify due to the familiarity of practice. Placing glory on a person for holy, healthy, or prosperous living is common. Praising a person's beautiful sonnet, sermon, or song are other familiar ways to shift glory from Jesus onto humankind.

May believers reject glory for humankind. Jesus gave his own righteous life as a ransom for our sinful lives under the authority of God. Father, Son, and Holy Spirit deserve glory alone.

Epaphroditus

Philippians {4:18} But I have all, and abound: I am full, having received of Epaphroditus the things [which were sent] from you, an odour of a sweet smell, a sacrifice acceptable, wellpleasing to God.

PAUL EXPLAINED TO THE PHILIPPIANS IN HIS LETTER THAT Epaphroditus was very eager to serve the Lord. The incentive for Epaphroditus was to serve Christ and Paul, knowing that Paul's incentive was to see the fruit of the lives won for Christ to increase God's kingdom.

Epaphroditus risked his life in sickness by bringing the gifts to Paul from the church in Philippi, and by bringing Paul's letter to the church in Philippi. God mercifully healed Epaphroditus. God used Epaphroditus to provide for Paul and the church in Philippi, and as a result, we can read the book of Philippians in our Bible.

Humbly and faithfully serving God requires much stamina and strategy. Church leaders, missionaries, and the like, both men and women, serve sacrificially with the incentive to grow the kingdom of God. Let us be sure to honor them, for theirs is a fragrant offering that God considers an acceptable sacrifice.

Paul encouraged all to honor people like Epaphroditus because they do good works for God under the leading of the Holy Spirit. Many are worthy of honor who faithfully serve the Lord, and it is good for us to give them the honor that they deserve. The giving of self for the sake of the kingdom of heaven merits honor for the person, but all glory and honor belong to God.

Gamaliel

Acts {5:34} Then stood there up one in the council, a Pharisee, named Gamaliel, a doctor of the law, had in reputation among all the people, and commanded to put the apostles forth a little space.

IT HAS LONG BEEN KNOWN THAT EXCELLENT TEACHERS have profound influence over their students. Teachers who patiently listen for effective communication will help their students make wise decisions when faced with a crossroad. Both teachers and students are to prepare to learn and to be taught.

The Apostle Paul was trained by a prominent rabbi, an influential teacher in the matters of what the Jews could and could not teach regarding God. Gamaliel was the voice of reason and relaxed the Jews who were ready to kill Peter and other followers of Jesus. The Christians were ordered not to teach in Jesus's name, but they continued teaching in Jerusalem.

Gamaliel wisely advised to let the Christian movement run its course. Historians will find it difficult to disagree with Gamaliel, if a movement is of man, it will phase out. Gamaliel learned and taught that historically, social movements cycle, and it is best not to risk going against God.

Whether a movement is reformative, revolutionary, resistance, or religious, the only way it will last is if God ordains it. The gospel was not a religious movement of man, it is of God. God moves people with faith in Jesus from a sinful destiny of death to eternal glory in heaven.

Shallun

*Nehemiah {3:15} But the gate of the fountain repaired
Shallun the son of Colhozeh, the ruler of part of
Mizpah; he built it, and covered it, and set up the doors
thereof, the locks thereof, and the bars thereof, and the
wall of the pool of Siloah by the king's garden, and unto
the stairs that go down from the city of David.*

IT IS EASY TO MARVEL AT THE HANDIWORK OF GOD. AMONG
many of God's intriguing innovations is the gathering of
waters such like for use in a fountain. Fountains overflow
with beauty for both practical and ornate purposes. Fountains are useful to life.

Shallun was under the leadership of Nehemiah, who was
heading up the effort to come and rebuild the gates and wall of
God's great city. Each wall and each gate needed careful notice.
The names of the men who helped are recorded in the Bible.

Rebuilding the Fountain Gate and the wall of the Pool
of Siloah was a special task, and Shallun gave this his special focus. These repairs were essential restorations to the
city. Shallun restored a life-giving feature to God's great
city of Jerusalem.

Jesus finished a special task that restored living water to
humanity. Water is the most essential element required for
life. Jesus restores the human heart so that a fountain of living
water can cleanse, sustain, and raise believers from the dead
in the power of the Spirit by the gift of faith.

Zadok

1 Kings {1:38} So Zadok the priest, and Nathan the prophet, and Benaiah the son of Jehoiada, and the Cherethites, and the Pelethites, went down, and caused Solomon to ride upon king David's mule, and brought him to Gihon. {1:39} And Zadok the priest took an horn of oil out of the tabernacle, and anointed Solomon. And they blew the trumpet; and all the people said, God save king Solomon.

WHEN CONFUSION, TURBULENCE, AND SETBACKS IN LIFE prevail, it is important to remember who you serve and how. Periods of disappointment can lead to an absence of drive. Feelings of dullness for service, temptation to envy, and a falling away from faith can all result from disappointment.

Zadok was a priest who experienced disappointments. In his service to King David, Zadok witnessed David's son Absalom's murderous plans. Zadok faithfully cared for the ark of the covenant during the difficult siege. Zadok saw an attack on the throne from David's son Adonijah, who held a great feast and declared himself king. Zadok knew that the next king was to be Solomon, so he and his people followed the king's orders and God's will by anointing Solomon as king.

Zadok was patient with disappointment, knowing God had a plan. Jesus was patient with God's plan for the cross. When disappointment sets in, remember that Jesus endured rejection from his own people who caused him suffering at the cross, so we may hope in eternal life. Jesus is no stranger to disappointment and offers hope for those who love him.

Jezebel

*1 Kings {19:1} And Ahab told Jezebel all that Elijah
had done, and withal how he had slain all the prophets
with the sword.*

JEZEBEL WAS THE PERSONIFICATION OF MALEVOLENCE.
Jezebel made life a terrifying place to live for the Israelites,
especially trying to terrify the prophet, Elijah. The queen's
first order of business was to usher in Baal worship to God's
people. Jezebel's second order of business was to murder all
the prophets of the God of the Jews. Elijah prayed that God
would send a severe drought.

Elijah invited 450 prophets of Baal to Mount Carmel for a
demonstration of power between the God of Israel and Baal.
The prophets prepared a bull for a sacrifice and called on Baal
from morning to noon to come and show power with fire to
accept the offering.

Baal was not going to answer, so Elijah acted. Elijah
repaired the altar of the Lord that was torn down, took twelve
stones, one for each of the tribes of the family of Jacob, put
the wood and bull on the altar, and had the prophets of Baal
fill the altar with water three times.

Elijah prayed and fire fell consuming the offering and
all the water. That day, God sent the rains back, the drought
was over, and afterward, Jezebel died. God protected Elijah
from Jezebel's terror of death and God protects Jesus's faithful
believers from sin's terror of death too. Jesus secures the end
of believers to eternal life by his love and sacrifice at the cross.

The Ethiopian Eunuch

Acts {8:27} And he arose and went: and, behold, a man of Ethiopia, an eunuch of great authority under Candace queen of the Ethiopians, who had the charge of all her treasure, and had come to Jerusalem for to worship.

THERE ARE MANY DIFFERENT ETHNICITIES AND SOCIAL statuses that create boundaries between people. Scripture teaches, however, that God divided humanity into two categories—Jew and Gentile. Jews are God's people set apart, whose lineage would be the Savior, and Gentiles were not. Gentiles were discriminated against by the Jews and regarded as unclean.

The Ethiopian eunuch would have been discriminated against as he was not only a Gentile but a Gentile in servitude. Still, the Ethiopian wished to worship, and the natural place to learn how to worship God is to read from his Word.

The Ethiopian eunuch needed help understanding the text he was reading, and Philip was led by the Lord to cross the boundaries of ethnicity and social status to help. Philip was able to help the Ethiopian eunuch to understand that that text was related to the good news of Jesus Christ. How Jesus was sent as a lamb of God to take away the sins of the world by death and resurrection for all who will believe.

The Ethiopian eunuch, a Gentile man, received God's free gift of faith that day and was baptized in the same way as all of the other Jewish converts. Jesus offers the gift of faith to all nations of the world. Jesus does not discriminate.

Chapter 14

1 Chronicles {16:23}
Sing unto the LORD,
all the earth;
shew forth from
day to day his salvation.

Jehosheba

2 Kings {11:2} But Jehosheba, the daughter of king Joram, sister of Ahaziah, took Joash the son of Ahaziah and stole him from among the king's sons [which were] slain; and they hid him, [even] him and his nurse, in the bedchamber from Athaliah, so that he was not slain.

NO ONE KNOWS WHEN THE ENEMY WILL STRIKE, SO IT IS important to be on the watch for danger, and to act wisely to preserve life. When King Joash was just one year old, his family was massacred by his wicked mother, Athaliah, so to secure her crown as Queen of Judah. Joash's aunt Jehosheba rescued Joash and hid him in the house of the Lord with her husband, Jehoiada.

When Joash was seven years old, he was brought out of hiding and crowned king of Judah. Jehosheba's husband, Jehoiada, became a leader to Joash, who did what was right.

Jehosheba watched for her opportunity to rescue King Joash for the greater good of God's people. Jehosheba's husband Jehoiada helped God's people to commit to God-honoring leadership. Jehoiada posted watchmen for protection and encouragement for the people to be wholly devoted to God. The watchman warned of the danger of turning away from God.

May we be hidden in Jesus, where the Spirit watches our heart and convicts us of sin, so we may act wisely and preserve life. Church leaders are our watchmen, as we are watchmen for those around us. No one knows when Jesus will return, so be on the watch today.

Jeremiah

*Jeremiah {29:10} For thus saith the LORD, That after
seventy years be accomplished at Babylon I will visit you,
and perform my good word toward you, in causing you
to return to this place. {29:11} For I know the thoughts
that I think toward you, saith the LORD, thoughts of
peace, and not of evil, to give you an expected end.*

GOD'S PEOPLE WERE CALLED TO LIVE HOLY LIVES WHILE
they waited for their Messiah; however, God's people repeatedly chose sin over purity. Jeremiah warned the southern
kingdom tribes of Judah and Benjamin to turn to God, and
repeatedly Jeremiah felt spiritually rejected.

Jeremiah wondered why his pain would not cease, why the
wound of his heart would not heal, why it seemed as though
God was failing in keeping his promises. Jeremiah was lonely
with no family, no friends, and a God who appeared to be
distant. God gave Jeremiah a promise of hope.

Jeremiah experienced a darkness that was overwhelming
because he understood the consequence of sin. Jeremiah was
determined to warn God's people to turn away from their
sin no matter how he was rejected. Seventy years after the
Babylon capture, God's people sought him. God returned
his nation to Jerusalem for restoration and reconciliation.
God keeps promises.

Jesus's light overcomes overwhelming darkness. Jesus
warns people to forsake sin and receive eternal life. Jesus
seeks those who want to be restored and reconciled to God
by righteousness. Believers can rejoice over the lives of both
Jeremiah and Jesus because God is a promise keeper.

Capernaum

Matthew {11:23} And thou, Capernaum, which art exalted unto heaven, shalt be brought down to hell: for if the mighty works, which have been done in thee, had been done in Sodom, it would have remained until this day.

THERE ARE SO MANY WORLD VIEWS. THERE IS SO MUCH TO see, so many people to follow, and so many observations to consider that one would be looking for truth forever without the lens of grace.

Jesus made his home in Capernaum for a while where he performed miracles and taught in the synagogues. Surely the people of Capernaum witnessed Jesus's supernatural activity, and gossip likely went around regarding his authentic Messianic signs. Capernaum should have been one of the first towns to hope in Jesus and give God glory, yet they rejected Jesus.

Capernaum and the other cities that rejected Jesus are a good reminder that our faith is a gift, and that not all who hear the gospel will ask for faith. Like Capernaum, many view the world through a selfish lens in hope of another means of salvation other than faith in Jesus.

God desires praise by means of redemption through the glorious work of Jesus. God places the desire for genuine belief in the human heart, so to give the gift of faith. There is a great mystery regarding human duty and God's sovereignty as they work together in God's plan for salvation.

May we never give up praying for the lost and sharing the love of Christ to all who will hear.

King Nebuchadnezzar

Daniel {4:33} The same hour was the thing fulfilled
upon Nebuchadnezzar: and he was driven from men,
and did eat grass as oxen, and his body was wet with
the dew of heaven, till his hairs were grown like eagles
[feathers,] and his nails like birds' [claws.]

EVERY SO OFTEN, A PERSON HAS THE ACCEPTABLE FEELING of pride in a job well done or in a loved one's accomplishments. Feeling pride in the Lord is a good thing; however, God hates selfish pride.

God used King Nebuchadnezzar of Babylonia to punish God's prideful people, who were steeped in idolatry. God warned the people by the prophets, but they did not listen. God gave the chosen people to Babylon in stages, with the result being exile, confiscation of God's temple treasures, the ruin of Jerusalem, and burning of the temple of the Lord, built by King Solomon.

King Nebuchadnezzar acquired Hebrews to serve in his kingdom. One of the men was Daniel, who could interpret dreams. Twice Daniel was called into the king's quarters to interpret difficult dreams. The first dream showed the king's power and strength in comparison to future kingdoms. The next dream was one that Daniel wished upon someone else because it showed King Nebuchadnezzar's penalty for his prideful desire for exaltation.

Nebuchadnezzar was humbled by God in the wilderness. Jesus was humbled by the shameful cross according to God's will; however, Jesus alone is worthy of exaltation. May we avoid selfish pride, so to be found proud only in Jesus's finished work at the cross and his will for our lives.

Ebed-melech

Jeremiah {38:8} Ebed-melech went forth out of the king's house, and spake to the king, saying, {38:9} My lord the king, these men have done evil in all that they have done to Jeremiah the prophet, whom they have cast into the dungeon; and he is like to die for hunger in the place where he is: for [there is] no more bread in the city. {38:10} Then the king commanded Ebed-melech the Ethiopian, saying, Take from hence thirty men with thee, and take up Jeremiah the prophet out of the dungeon, before he die.

WHEN OBSERVING THE NIGHT SKY, ONE WILL NOTICE THAT it is always darkest after dusk and just before the dawn. Dawn still has darkness; however, the hope of bright light in the morning sun is sure.

Ebed-melech witnessed one of God's prophets face a desperate time of darkness. Jeremiah was proclaiming God's message to the southern kingdom of Judah, and he was censored and imprisoned for it. God's people were warned that Babylon was to capture them and destroy their city as a punishment for their love for their sin.

Ebed-melech was one of the few spots of dawn in the life of Jeremiah. Ebed-melech grieved knowing Jeremiah was in the pit, left to die, so he headed up a compassionate rescue plan. Like Ebed-melech was a bright light to Jeremiah, Jesus is a bright light that brings sinners out of the pit of dark death by grace and mercy. Jesus's compassionate rescue plan was the plan of the cross.

Laban

Genesis {31:26} And Laban said to Jacob, What hast thou done, that thou hast stolen away unawares to me, and carried away my daughters, as captives [taken] with the sword? {31:27} Wherefore didst thou flee away secretly, and steal away from me; and didst not tell me, that I might have sent thee away with mirth, and with songs, with tabret, and with harp?

DEEP IN THE HEART OF HUMANKIND IS THE DESIRE TO BE an authority like God. People want to decide the fate of others, to judge self-righteously, and to be known as a blessing. Only God can bless, and he sometimes uses unlikely people in his will.

Laban was the tricky father-in-law of the trickster Jacob. Jacob fled to Laban for fear of his brother Esau because he stole his Messianic blessing upon the deathbed of their father. Even before that, Jacob persuaded his brother to verbally sell his birthright for a bowl of beans.

Jacob worked hard for Laban, and God prospered Laban. Livestock, children, and the yielding of the earth made Laban a rich man. When Jacob gained some wealth for himself, he fell out of favor with the prideful Laban, so he fled. Laban pursued Jacob for all that was stolen.

Laban caught Jacob, but released him, with his blessing, out of fear of Jacob's God. Laban's daughter Rachel was mother to Joseph, who saved God's people from starvation. Laban's daughter Leah was mother to Judah, of the direct lineage of Jesus. Trust God's wisdom to use anyone to accomplish his will.

Mary Magdalene

John {20:16} Jesus saith unto her, Mary. She turned herself,
and saith unto him, Rabboni; which is to say, Master.

THERE IS SUCH A COMFORT IN HAVING COMPANIONSHIP.
Having a trusted friend to talk to when times are sad, when
times are good, or when times are just average is priceless.
When you find a friend who shows you how much he or she
cares about you, you never forget. Finding a good friend who
is willing to stand by your side is rare in this world.

Mary from Magdala had a friend like this in Jesus. Mary
was healed by Jesus from demonic possession. Out of her
love for Jesus, she helped to provide for needs, followed to
the foot of the cross, and then to the empty tomb. Mary was
heartbroken, and not satisfied with the rushed burial of her
Lord before the Passover. Mary was determined to anoint
Jesus, to give a proper burial according to Jewish custom.

As Mary approached Jesus's tomb she did not expect to
see her friend resurrected from the dead. All Jesus had to do
was call Mary's name and her sorrow was turned into joy. The
Bible says that God's people recognize his voice, and Mary
recognized the voice of the Savior.

During a time when women were regarded as unreliable
witnesses, Jesus appeared first to his friend Mary. The Father
gives believers faith in Jesus, and a comforting friend to stand
by our side for life, who is the Holy Spirit. Do you recognize
the voice of Jesus?

Onesiphorus

2 Timothy {1:16} The Lord give mercy unto the house of Onesiphorus; for he oft refreshed me, and was not ashamed of my chain. {2:3} Thou therefore endure hardness, as a good soldier of Jesus Christ.

PRISONERS AND SOLDIERS AROUND THE WORLD ALL EXPErience a different level of confinement. Some survive a limited time due to poor circumstances, and some actually experience a better life than they had prior to their confinement. A person will either volunteer as a prisoner/soldier to Jesus, or a prisoner/soldier to sin.

The Apostle Paul was a prisoner for Jesus who experienced both difficulty and hope. Many followers of Jesus fearfully turned away because of the authorities. Onesiphorus was a faithful follower who refused to fall away and refused glory for himself for all he did.

Onesiphorus is worthy of emulating in his role of the faithful Christian soldier, unashamed of the chains of Christ. Paul was blessed by the earnest nature of Onesiphorus to diligently do God's will. Like Onesiphorus sought Paul to minister to him and provide comfort, the Spirit of God also seeks Jesus's faithful to minister to and provide comfort for.

Prisoners and soldiers of Jesus diligently pursue God's will at any cost. Prisoners and soldiers of sin turn glory away from God onto themselves. Following Jesus requires doing God's will for God's glory. Resist seeking glory for yourself when doing a service for God. Keep your heart from pride and diligently take your marching orders from the Bible, so that you may do God's will for God's glory.

Amaziah

Amos {7:12} Also Amaziah said unto Amos, O thou seer, go, flee thee away into the land of Judah, and there eat bread, and prophesy there.

MANY SEEK TO DEFINE TRUTH BASED ON THEIR CHOSEN source, and that source changes frequently. The world views truth as subjective. Truth must not be based on the source of individual preference; however, all around the world, human emotion is trusted to determine the truth from error.

Individuals who search for their own truth apart from the truth offered by the Word of God will one day be faced with the Creator of the world and the author of truth. These individuals are easy to recognize because they refuse truth, follow their pliable hearts, and reject God.

Amaziah was a priest of God, but he rejected the truth of God. Amaziah did not want to deliver the prophet Amos's message of truth to the king because the message was terrible. God's chosen nation was to be judged for its rebelliousness and they did not want to hear it.

Like many people today, Amaziah refused truth, resolved to lie, and advanced doom on God's chosen people. Israel spent seventy years captive to a pagan nation.

As time passes, more believers will hear advice like Amaziah gave to Amos, "Go away and prophesy somewhere else." Helping others to discern truth from error can be a difficult and lonely task; however, Jesus promises to never leave us alone. Jesus is the high priest of God; he is the truth of God, and scripture never changes.

Onesimus

Philemon {1:10} I beseech thee for my son Onesimus, whom I
have begotten in my bonds: {1:11} Which in time past was to
thee unprofitable, but now profitable to thee and to me.

THERE ARE FEW THINGS MORE ABHORRENT THAN FORCED
slavery. Many were sold into slavery, either by themselves
or their families, so to meet economic needs. Sadly, forced
slavery exists today.

Slavery in the Bible was not based on ethnicity, but on
economic status. Slaves were afforded justice, with hope
for loving lords, and emancipation, according to God's law.
Humans are either slaves to Jesus for eternal life or slaves to
sin that leads to death.

Onesimus was a slave who escaped his master and had
a life-changing encounter with the Apostle Paul. As a new
Christian, Onesimus was conscientious to be obedient and
do the right thing by honoring God's law. In a letter to Onesimus's master, Paul reminded of Jesus's restoration of lost sinful
humanity to God for the purpose of good works.

Paul offered to make things right by paying Onesimus's
debt in full, and pleaded for emancipation, so Onesimus
could serve the Lord as a free man. Onesimus could only
freely perform the work of the Lord by serving Paul if he were
set free from his master's binding debt.

Praise God for Jesus Christ who paid our sin debt in full
at the cross to purchase us out of slavery to sin and death.
Humans can never know God's wisdom or reconcile something as sickening as forced slavery to evil, human lords;
however, believers can know that God is always good.

Micah

Judges {17:10} And Micah said unto him, Dwell with me, and be unto me a father and a priest, and I will give thee ten [shekels] of silver by the year, and a suit of apparel, and thy victuals. So the Levite went in.

IT IS SAFE TO SAY THAT WHEN PARENTS DO NOT EQUIP themselves with necessary parenting tools, their children will likely not grow up to become their best version in adulthood. The conscience needs training, and every parent must raise children well using their best resource, which is the Bible.

Micah was a child whose mother was not utilizing God's truth to instruct her son to know right from wrong. After returning silver he stole from his mother, he followed her direction to practice idolatry and did so into his adulthood. Micah's conscience started off well toward God as he knew stealing was wrong. Micah's heart grew far from God and his adulthood was an apostasy.

Although God was not a priority, God was remembered. Micah enjoyed his carved images, his shrine, his ephod, and even ordained one of his sons to be his priest. Knowing only Levites could be true priests, Micah took advantage of an opportunity to persuade a Levite to reside with him.

Micah's adulthood reminds that youth must be trained to discern good from evil. Fostering a love for Jesus will help children grow up and not depart from God's will. A team effort of believers willing to read God's Word and share their knowledge with the next generation is vital.

The Tower of Babel

*Genesis {11:9} Therefore is the name of it called Babel;
because the LORD did there confound the language
of all the earth: and from thence did the LORD scatter
them abroad upon the face of all the earth.*

WITHOUT GOD, HUMANKIND WILL DO NOTHING BUT BAD all the time. God demonstrated this in the account of Noah. God's fresh start with Noah came with directions, multiply and fill the earth. Noah's descendants refused to follow God's direction because they were independent and proud.

God scattered the nations because of the prideful work at the tower of Babel. Noah's descendants were working out their own plan to reach heaven with baked bricks and mortar, so to make themselves famous. God caused the people to develop into a global, cultural phenomenon so that Jesus Christ could gather them together forever in holiness. May God's faithful not allow independent pride and works to be the building blocks to climb to heaven. The reward for the proud and independent heart is contrary to the reward for those who hope in Jesus.

Consider Jesus's parable of the wise and foolish builders found in Matthew 7:24-27. The wise man builds on the rock of Jesus and his house stands firm when challenged by the elements. The foolish man builds on the sand, the wisdom of the world, and his house does not stand firm because it lacks a true foundation. May believers trust in Jesus alone for forgiveness of sins, otherwise we will try to work our way to heaven and fail.

Abishag

1 Kings {2:22} And king Solomon answered and said unto his mother, And why dost thou ask Abishag the Shunammite for Adonijah? ask for him the kingdom also; for he [is] mine elder brother.

THE CHANGING OF A DYNASTY, A PRESIDENCY, OR LEADER-ship can create a sense of anxiety and worry. When power exchanges hands, remember that God is in control.

Abishag was a witness to a powerful exchange of leader-ship that was decreed by God. King David was old, close to death, and needed someone to tend to him regularly. King David's servants suggested that they locate a woman to serve him, to keep him warm, and care for him. Abishag was a virtuous Shulamite who attended to the king and remained pure.

David's son Adonijah publicly pronounced himself as king of Israel, so King David appointed Solomon as king while he was still alive to see it. Adonijah was fearful for his life for declaring his father's throne; however, Solomon spared his life. In another effort to take the throne as king of Israel, as the older brother, Adonijah tried one more devious tactic. Adonijah attempted and failed to marry his father's concubine, Abishag.

Abishag witnessed a struggle for an exchange of power firsthand and likely worried about her future in the royal family. Like Abishag, believers patiently wait for God's will during transfers of governing authorities. Faithful believers find comfort in knowing that King Jesus promises to never leave his royal family. God has a plan for every transition of power in the world.

Hephzibah

*Isaiah {62:2} And the Gentiles shall see thy righteous-
ness, and all kings thy glory: and thou shalt be called
by a new name, which the mouth of the LORD shall
name. {62:4} Thou shalt no more be termed Forsaken;
neither shall thy land any more be termed Desolate:
but thou shalt be called Hephzi-bah, and thy land
Beulah: for the LORD delighteth in thee.*

HEPHZIBAH WAS THE NAME OF THE WIFE OF GOOD KING
Hezekiah, and her name means "My delight is in her." Hephzibah's root word, hafz, suggests that Queen Hephzibah
was not only a delight but also guarded and protected. The
meaning of a name was especially important in Bible times,
and when God changed the name of a person or a land, it was
significant. Hephzibah was also the name given to Israel out
of God's great love and grace, despite its constant sin cycle.

Consider the parable of the prodigal son found in Luke
15:11-32. The son turned away from his father and broke his
heart. The prodigal returned destitute to his father with the
hope of being treated like a servant. The prodigal is welcomed
back immediately by the father with open arms and no questions asked. This is the love God has for his children.

Jesus desires to forgive you and to call you Hephzibah
too. Jesus seeks to delight in you forever, to bless you, protect you, guard you, and reconcile you. Jesus knows our sin
nature is like the prodigal son, yet still loves us. May Jesus
call us Hephzibah.

Chapter 15

———◈✦◈———

Luke {13:18}
Then said he, Unto what is the
kingdom of God like?
and whereunto shall I resemble it?
{13:19} It is like a grain
of mustard seed, which a man took,
and cast into his garden; and it grew,
and waxed a great tree;
and the fowls of the air lodged in the branches of it.

Zelophehad

Numbers {27:7} The daughters of Zelophehad speak right: thou shalt surely give them a possession of an inheritance among their father's brethren; and thou shalt cause the inheritance of their father to pass unto them.

A LAND INHERITANCE WAS ESPECIALLY IMPORTANT TO THE Israelites. Specific laws applied to the ownership of land to provide for the security for the tribes of Israel. When it was finally time for Israel to inherit its land, God divided it up accordingly and made sure to make provisions, so that the land would not be inherited by strangers in the future.

The trouble for Zelophehad's daughters was that their father died in the wilderness, and they had no brother to inherit the land. The inheritance law would leave them destitute. Zelophehad's daughter bravely brought her grievance for herself and her clan to the tent of the meeting to discuss the matter before the people.

The ruling brought about a more specific strategy to distribute the wealth of inheritance. God provided a new model for the distribution of inheritance that expanded the rights of women. When a son was not available to receive an inheritance, the daughters would receive it.

Jesus made it possible for believers to have a secure inheritance because of his perfect life and redemptive work on the cross. Jesus's physical resurrection confirms the promised inheritance for the faithful people regardless of gender or ethnicity. One day, the faithful will live in heaven with God, in our glorious bodies that are free from sin forever.

Barak

Judges {4:8} And Barak said unto her, If thou wilt go with me, then I will go: but if thou wilt not go with me, [then] I will not go.

SOCIETY CHALLENGES THE ROLES OF MEN AND WOMEN, often in a way that does not bring God glory. For many, this differentiation is a source of frustration because they seek to challenge God's order of creation.

Historically, men have been stronger when it comes to the battlefield and in the administration of justice; however, that was not always the case. God uses women too.

Barak was a military leader who was confident in the female judge, Deborah. Barak would trust God's plan for war on one condition, Deborah was to join him. Deborah trusted God to lead.

God gave the glory for the victory to a woman named Jael, who pierced the trusting enemy's temple with a tent peg until he died. Sometimes God will work around cowardly men who refuse to do God's will by circumventing responsibility to women who are willing to serve.

The temptation for women in ministry to equate themselves with their male counterparts can lead to a dishonorable service. Scripture is clear that women who follow Jesus reject the exercise of spiritual leadership over men in public ministry. May we trust God in his wisdom for public ministry.

Barak reminds that Jesus is glorified when men and women serve together. Barak was a leader who was glad to give glory to God for his strong female counterparts. Both Deborah and Jael praised God for their strength in the Lord.

Pisgah

Deuteronomy {34:1} And Moses went up from the plains of Moab unto the mountain of Nebo, to the top of Pisgah, that [is] over against Jericho. And the LORD shewed him all the land of Gilead, unto Dan.

SIN HAS A WAY OF CREEPING IN SLOWLY AND TAKING UP unwelcomed residency. For the faithful follower of Jesus, the situation of living for sin will take away fellowship and blessings that the Lord wishes to bestow. The human condition is as inclined to sin as a sparrow is inclined to fly. So often, people do not realize the effect of their sin until it is too late.

Many people struggle with many different sinful patterns. Some patterns are less obvious than others. Either way, sinful patterns in God's faithful yield disastrous consequences. Pisgah was a place that God used to judge a sinful pattern of angry disobedience.

In Meribah, God commanded Moses to speak to a rock to allow the people to receive a blessing of flowing water. The people were again unhappy and complained of their thirst. Unfortunately, Moses yielded to his anger and struck the rock while yelling at the people, disobeying God.

Moses did not step foot in the promised land because he went to be with God, but first God showed him what he lost from Pisgah. Pisgah reminds that sin separates servants of Jesus Christ from fully knowing all of God's blessings. May the faithful never see a place like Pisgah, where Jesus shows our loss due to our sinful patterns.

Kore

2 Chronicles {31:14} And Kore the son of Imnah the Levite, the porter toward the east, [was] over the freewill offerings of God, to distribute the oblations of the LORD, and the most holy things.

WHAT DO ALL THE NATIONS OF THE WORLD CRAVE? FREE-dom. From the beginning of time, humans have sought freedom. Humans want the freedom to choose what they want to do, when they want to do it. With the benefaction of freedom comes great responsibility.

King Ahaz offered sacrifices to pagan gods because he believed they would help him. Israel suffered as a result. Ahaz's successor, King Hezekiah, was a good king who reunited God's people to God. King Hezekiah reinstated the Passover, removed idols, and encouraged God's people to freely give generously to bless the priests.

Kore was a witness of what seemed like a miraculous turn of events. God's people were offered the freedom to reconcile their hearts to God through holy offerings and they did so phenomenally. The free will offering given by God's loving people was so overwhelming that Kore needed six assistants to distribute to every single priest and their families. Kore also witnessed God's people using their freedom to consecrate themselves to the Lord.

Followers of Jesus are free from the penalty of sin, so they may freely offer God their bodies as a living sacrifice without condemnation. Righteous deeds done for God's glory are not enough to satisfy God's wrath against personal sin. Leaders today rejoice like Kore when believers use their freedoms faithfully.

Sceva

Acts {19:14} And there were seven sons of [one] Sceva,
a Jew, [and] chief of the priests, which did so.
{19:15} And the evil spirit answered and said, Jesus I
know, and Paul I know; but who are ye?

MYSTERIOUS PROMISES, SIGNS, AND WONDERS ARE FASCI-
nating to many. There are people all over the world who claim
to have understanding regarding spiritual books, items, or
powers far exceeding the average person. Some claim that
they can receive messages from human spirits who have
passed away, some declare that they can see the future, and
some profess that they are healers.

Sceva was a high priest with seven sons who were involved
with paranormal activity. Sceva's sons saw the disciples of
Jesus doing extraordinary miracles in the name of Jesus and
pursued similar success. Sceva's sons falsely claimed the power
of Jesus to heal a man by removing an evil spirit and that spirit
tried to destroy them. The spirit world is real and dangerous.

Like the sons of Sceva, many churches claim to minister
in Jesus's name. These churches alter the gospel with lies like
the greater the person's faith the greater their healing, or the
greater the person's giving the greater their prosperity. Some
misrepresent Christ's finished work on the cross by demanding people sacrificially give and do works.

Deuteronomy 18 forbids communicating with the deceased,
or speaking a false prophecy, so beware of the paranormal.
Trust in Jesus and the Bible as God's absolute best source for
communication between our spirit and the Holy Spirit.

The First Woman

1 Kings {3:24} And the king said, Bring me a sword. And
they brought a sword before the king. {3:25} And the
king said, Divide the living child in two, and give half
to the one, and half to the other. {3:26} Then spake the
woman whose the living child [was] unto the king, for
her bowels yearned upon her son, and she said, O my
lord, give her the living child, and in no wise slay it.

THERE ARE FEW WORSE FEELINGS THAN BEING UP AGAINST
a liar who cannot be proven wrong. When a judge is faced
with two convincing versions, only one of which is correct,
they tend to consider the balance of probabilities and genu-
ineness of both parties.

King Solomon received wisdom from God. In one case
King Solomon judged between two women alone in a home,
each with an infant boy, one living and one dead. The first
woman accused the other of switching the infants in the night.
The mother of the dead baby killed him with her weight while
asleep. The other woman accused the first woman of the same
crime, claiming the living baby was hers.

King Solomon knew that the probability was low for a
loving mother to approve of the execution of her baby. The
evidence of the genuine love of the first woman for her baby
was proof that she was the mother and justice prevailed.

Like the first woman had hope in King Solomon's wisdom
to judge righteously, we have the same hope in King Jesus.
Jesus is the wise judge who delivers perfect justice by his
righteousness, and none can prove him wrong.

Eunice

2 Timothy {1:5} When I call to remembrance the unfeigned faith that is in thee, which dwelt first in thy grandmother Lois, and thy mother Eunice; and I am persuaded that in thee also.

ADULT INTERACTIONS AND HABITS ARE ALL BEING observed by children and youth, leaving an imprint on their hearts and minds. Those imprints will help to shape and mold children into who they will become as adults. Children will either model good and godly behavior or they will revolt. God gives every human free will to choose Jesus or to not choose Jesus.

Eunice was Timothy's mother. Eunice, along with Timothy's grandmother Lois, taught Timothy about God's Word, God's holiness, the sin condition, the need for God's forgiveness, and the coming Messiah who would save them. Eunice prepared Timothy's heart to receive faith in Jesus when he heard the gospel. Eunice cultivated the heart of her son, the Apostle Paul planted the seed, and God gave Timothy the increase of faith. Eunice was a woman who feared the Lord.

Eunice is a good example of a godly mother who instructed her son about Jesus. Timothy worked as a leader in his local church and confidently and accurately shared the gospel with people, so to grow the kingdom. Nurturing children in love, discipline, and in the Lord will help their hearts to be prepared to receive faith in Christ when it is God's appointed time. Studying the Bible with children helps them to become adults equipped to present themselves as workers for Jesus.

The Two-Drachma Tax Collectors

Matthew {17:27} Notwithstanding, lest we should offend them, go thou to the sea, and cast an hook, and take up the fish that first cometh up; and when thou hast opened his mouth, thou shalt find a piece of money: that take, and give unto them for me and thee.

SEVERAL PEOPLE ARE QUOTED AS SAYING: "THERE ARE TWO things in life that will certainly be counted on, they are death and taxes." The law of Moses required that an annual census take place and that one-half shekel be collected as a temple tax from every Jew over the age of twenty years.

The two-drachma tax collectors questioned why Jesus and Peter did not pay their tax. Jesus explained to Peter that the Son of the King should be tax-exempt. In the same miraculous manner that God used a big fish to deliver Jonah to his destination, God used a little fish to deliver a shekel to pay the temple tax for himself and Peter. Jesus was more focused on the cross.

For those who hope in Jesus, there are two things in life that will certainly be counted on, they are God's law and gospel. Law reveals holiness and gospel satisfies God's wrath against sin. Children of the king are not taxed by the king, so believers can know that salvation is not for those who follow the law, pay their taxes, and do good works. Salvation is not something earned or purchased. Salvation is the miraculous gift of God's grace, to believers by faith in Jesus.

Romans {10:12} For there is no difference between the Jew and the Greek: for the same Lord over all is rich unto all that call upon him. {10:13} For whosoever shall call upon the name of the Lord shall be saved.

The Shofar

Joel {2:1} Blow ye the trumpet in Zion, and sound an
alarm in my holy mountain: let all the inhabitants of
the land tremble: for the day of the LORD cometh,
for [it is] nigh at hand.

LOUD NOISES HAVE A WAY OF CATCHING THE ATTENTION
of people and can invoke feelings of either pleasure or despair.

On the seventh month, on the first day, God's people
would celebrate a day of rest that was ushered in by a loud
noise from a trumpet horn. A food offering was the only work
allowed on that solemn day, when God's people would repent,
self-examine, and worship God.

Yom Teruah is a holiday known as the day of the trumpets,
where God's people celebrate by blowing the shofar trumpet,
a call to repent. The noise of the shofar is to be received with
pleasure for those who are eternally secure in God or received
in despair for those who are not.

Ten days after the blast of the shofar was the Day of
Atonement, where the priests would sacrifice for the sins of
themselves and for the sins of God's people.

When Jesus returns, at the last sound of the trumpet, the
sinful flesh that once required daily sanctification will become
glorified like Jesus. Dishonorable flesh that never received the
gift of faith to salvation will experience despair at the sound of
God's trumpet call. May our noise of the gospel cause a vibra-
tion that gets the attention of the lost, to win hearts to Jesus.

The Poor Widow

*Matthew {6:19} Lay not up for yourselves treasures
upon earth, where moth and rust doth corrupt, and
where thieves break through and steal: {6:20} But lay
up for yourselves treasures in heaven, where neither
moth nor rust doth corrupt, and where thieves do not
break through nor steal: {6:21} For where your treasure
is, there will your heart be also.*

HEALTHY RELATIONSHIPS ARE A NECESSITY FOR A HAPPY
life because they fulfill a fundamental basic need for people,
which is love. People need to love and to feel loved. Healthy
relationships yield great joy and support. Healthy relationships are more important than social status or possessions.

We lay up for ourselves treasures in heaven by trusting
Jesus completely. The poor widow in Mark 12:41–44 lived
for the glory of God. The widow gave all she had, two copper
coins, the equivalent of a penny. In relation to the large sums
given by the wealthy people, her gift seemed insignificant.
Jesus stated that the widow's gift exceeded the total amount
that day at the treasury. The reason her gift was superior was
because the widow trusted God's ability to care for her needs,
over and above trusting money to care for her needs.

May we learn and grow in the power of the Holy Spirit to
be like the poor widow, who trusted and loved God more than
money. Let us not trust in or love the wealth of this world, but
to remember that our riches are found in the glory of Jesus.
May we cultivate healthy relationships with money and people,
so that our joy is found in the Lord, who is the author of love.

Barabbas

Mark {15:13} And they cried out again, Crucify him.
{15:14} Then Pilate said unto them, Why, what evil
hath he done? And they cried out the more exceedingly,
Crucify him. {15:15} And [so] Pilate, willing to content
the people, released Barabbas unto them, and delivered
Jesus, when he had scourged [him,] to be crucified.

TRADE-OFFS ARE INTERESTING TO WITNESS. SETTING ONE object free in exchange for the acquisition of another requires planning, consideration, and hope.

Just before Passover, the Jewish leaders rallied the people to turn against Jesus because of his declaration to be the Son of God. Pilate was put in a difficult position for his conscience. If Pilate did not honor the wishes of the Jewish mob, then he was at risk of ruining his political position regarding Caesar. If Pilate ordered the crucifixion of Jesus, then he would be guilty of murdering what he knew to be an innocent man. Pilate chose to honor the mob and keep his position by trading Jesus to go to the cross for Barabbas's freedom.

Jesus took the place of Barabbas on the cross. Barabbas was set free to live with no condemnation because this was God's will for him. Barabbas did nothing to earn his pardon from the death sentence. Barabbas was a trade-off to the Jews for the death of Jesus. Barabbas's sinful life was spared, and Jesus's holy body perished in his place because Jesus's role was to be the ultimate trade-off. God's final trade-off was the exchange of Jesus's life for your freedom.

The Widow of Zarephath

1 Kings {17:12} And she said, [As] the LORD thy God liveth, I have not a cake, but an handful of meal in a barrel, and a little oil in a cruse: and, behold, I [am] gathering two sticks, that I may go in and dress it for me and my son, that we may eat it, and die.

WHEN INDIVIDUALS PLACE THEIR TRUST IN ANYTHING BUT God, it is likely that they will succumb to discouragement. The widow of Zarephath was discouraged. God punished his people for Baal worship with a drought that spanned the entire Canaanite region.

God instructed Elijah to go to drought-plagued Sidon where an unknowing widow would feed him. Upon arrival, Elijah found the widow and asked her for a drink and a morsel of bread.

Elijah advised the widow that the Lord said that if she would make him a portion first and then make her meal, the jar of flour and the jug of oil would not run out until the Lord would send the rain. The widow believed and obeyed. Neither the jar of flour nor the jug of oil ran out.

Soon after, an illness came on the widow's son and he died. In grief and guilt of conscience, the widow accused Elijah of the tragedy, so he prayed to God for a miracle and Elijah brought him back to life. The widow confessed her genuine faith in God to Elijah.

Jesus seeks faith like that of the widow in Zarephath in obedience and confession.

Thomas

*John {20:29} Jesus saith unto him, Thomas, because
thou hast seen me, thou hast believed: blessed [are]
they that have not seen, and [yet] have believed.*

THE HUMAN HOPE FOR ETERNAL LIFE CAME AT A GREAT
price for God and people have free will to trust in Jesus or
to reject him.

Thomas was a loyal disciple to Jesus, even following when
their lives were in danger. Thomas's friends revealed that they
saw the risen Jesus. Thomas would not believe unless he saw
and touched Jesus's nail-pierced hands and side.

Thomas was granted his peace of mind. The struggle for
control over Thomas's mind and heart to believe in the risen
Savior was eliminated. Jesus offered Thomas the condition of
his experiment, to examine Jesus for himself. Thomas's experience with Jesus led him to be among the first to recognize
and confess that Jesus is God.

Hebrews 11:1 confirms the struggle to believe in something
that you cannot see for yourself. People have free will to believe
or not because God desires genuine relationships. When people
believe and ask Jesus for faith, he is faithful to give.

Jesus is the true link of the Holy Bible from cover to
cover. The Bible's recorded history, fulfilled prophecies, attributes, fulfilled promises, and preservation, despite countless
attempts to eliminate it, all prove it to be true. Let us make
every effort to know the gospel and share the gospel with ease
and accuracy. Faith comes by hearing God's Word.

Jesus's Throne

Psalm {93:2} Thy throne [is] established of old:
thou [art] from everlasting.

GOD HAS ESTABLISHED BOTH HIS THRONE AND THE thrones of humankind. The throne is the place where the greatest in command is seated, where there is the execution of law and judgment. Regardless of who is seated, we must always remember that God is in control.

The human throne is temporary, always needing a successor. The human throne shows partial judgment that can result in resentment, such as with King David's handling of his son Amnon. Amnon grossly mishandled his emotions and ruined his sister Tamar's life. In revenge, Tamar's brother Absalom murdered Amnon. Humanity needs a throne that delivers perfect justice.

Since the beginning of time, God promised to send the Messiah to recuse humankind from the judgment of sin. Redemptive promises were made and kept throughout the Old and the New Testament.

God chose the throne of King David, an imperfect, prideful, sinful king with a heart of love and repentance toward God. King David's throne was established by the Father for the Son to reign from forever.

God eliminated the temporary throne of humankind. Believers look forward to a spiritual kingdom consisting of a new heaven and a new earth, where righteousness dwells and where Jesus reigns.

Revelation {21:5} And he that sat upon the throne said, Behold, I make all things new.

The end.

Thank you for reading this daily devotional!
I pray it was a blessing to this season of your life
and that you are secure in your faith in Jesus.

If you are still not secure in your faith in Jesus,
I pray that you will continue to ask questions and
seek Jesus in the Holy Bible.

If you are looking for answers to your Bible questions,
I would like to recommend the website gotquestions.org.
The ESV Study Bible has wonderful study notes too.

Index

Made in the USA
Coppell, TX
26 August 2023

20823134R00148